Norma's blog gives me [...] workplace interactions can sometimes go off course, and how having a system and a resource to handle the inevitable bumps in the road can be a benefit. She is creative and funny in her description of scenarios about subject matter that isn't always funny.

>Renée Bates, Artist & President of The Chestnut Group
>(Plein Air Painters for the Land)

I SO enjoy your posts and your blogs. They are always smart (like you!) and I love your jungle brand.

>Amy Lynch, Speaker, Consultant, Author
>Generational Edge

Norma has the ability to provide practical insights to leaders in a conversational way. Her expertise helps leaders navigate the legal requirements of employee life yet also supports the kind of culture every business needs today.

>Kayla Barrett Curry, CEO
>Organization Impact, LLC

I love receiving the latest HR mystery from the HR Compliance Jungle blog. Norma Shirk's humor and light touch make swallowing the pill of dealing with messy HR issues much more palatable.

>Susan Hammonds-White, EdD, LPC/MHSP
>Lifecycles Counseling Services

Norma brings to life challenging work situations that arise for small business owners and HR professionals. Her characterizations are compelling, her humor is delightful and her advice is sound. I can highly recommend Norma as a valuable and trusted HR advisor.

    Kacky Fell

    Hatcher & Fell Photography

Norma - I love these! I really look forward to getting them.

    JB Palmer, REALTOR ®/Team Leader

    Keller Williams Realty Mount Juliet

PSYCHO BOSSES AND OBNOXIOUS CO-WORKERS

Surviving the HR Compliance Jungle

Norma Shirk

Copyright © 2018 by Norma Shirk

All rights reserved. No part of this book may be reproduced, stored in a retrieval system, or transmitted in any form or by any means—electronic, mechanical, photocopy, recording, or any other—except in the case of brief quotations embodied in critical articles and reviews, without the prior permission of the publisher.

For information contact: norma@complianceriskadvisor.com
or visit: www.hrcompliancejungle.com

Books by Norma Shirk may be purchased for educational, business or sales promotional use.
For information please write Corporate Compliance Risk Advisor, Attn: Norma Shirk, P. O. Box 295, Hermitage, TN 37076, or visit us at www.complianceriskadvisor.com.

Library of Congress Control Number: 2018956318

FIRST EDITION
Psycho Bosses and Obnoxious Co-Workers – 1st ed.

Print Version ISBN 978-1-7324885-1-9
eBook Version ISBN 978-1-7324885-0-2

Corporate Compliance Risk Advisor
P.O. 295
Hermitage, TN 37076
www.corporatecomplianceriskadvisor

Although the author and publisher have made every effort to provide accurate, up-to-date information, they accept no responsibility for loss, injury, or inconvenience sustained by any person reading or quoting this book.

Distributed by CCRA Press
www.ccra-press.com

CCRA PRESS

*To everyone who gave me material for this book,
whether they meant to or not.*

Contents

Introduction 9

PSYCHO BOSSES

Psycho Boss	The Lizard 12
You Want To Do What?	The Crow................... 15
I Don't Have a Drinking Problem	Lemmings 18
I'm In Charge!	The Wolverine 21
How Did I Get Into This Mess?	The Cape Buffalo............. 24
I've Had It with You!	The Warthog 27
Masters of The Universe	Peacocks................... 30
Working With a Jerk	The Weasel.................. 33
Mentor, Schmentor	The Hyena.................. 35
My Boss Hates Me!	The Rhino 38
Promoted To Failure	The Wasp................... 41
Let Me Do It!	The Magpie 44
The Peter Principle Strikes Again	The Sheep 47
Act Your Age!	The Tasmanian Devil 50
What'd You Say?	The Guinea Pig 53

OBNOXIOUS CO-WORKERS

Why Was I So Nice To The Punk?	The Rattlesnake 58
Sharing Sharon	The Chicken 61
Go Back To Your Cave	The Cockroach 64
Chaos Cathy	The Rat 67
The Knife In The Back	The Cobra 70
Queen Bee	The Bee 73
Me! Me! Me!	The Pig 76
The Back Stabber	The Coyote 79

I Thought We Were Friends	The Scorpion 82
Back Off!	The Giraffe 85
Have I Got a Deal for You!	The Weasel. 88
It Rhymes With Witch	The Skunk 91
New Job; Old Baggage	The Whitetail Deer 94
Make Her Go Away!	The Donkey. 97

OFFICE ROMANCES

Looking For Love	The Baboon 102
Will He Or Won't He?	The Tiger 105
The Morning After	The Tiger Cub 107
See, What Happened Was…	The Otters 110

MILENNIALS

Can We Get By Without Her?	The Lizard 114
Hey, Y'all, I'd Like a Job	The Puppy 117
Welcome To The Real World	The Squirrel. 120
I Want My Dream Job!	The Blind Mole 123
The Not-So-Little Prince	The Gazelle 126
Improving Morale With Beatings	The Long Horn Cattle 129

HOLIDAY HANGOVERS

Spring Fever	The Robin 134
April Fools. Not.	The Wolf 137
What Did You Do This Weekend?	The Sloth. 140
The Morning After	The Grizzly Bear 142
What Are You Wearing?	The Toucan 145
Happy Veterans Day!	The Bald Eagle. 148
Seasonal Slush And The Office Party	The Wildebeest 150
Acknowledgements	 152
Author Biography	 153

Introduction

Most books about human resources or HR issues are training manuals or moralistic tales of all the things one shouldn't do because they are prohibited by law. This HR book is not like that. This book is about the absurdity of human behavior.

Have you ever been forced to share a cubicle wall with a slob or a loudmouth? Or watched a crazy boss lose his or her grip on reality? Maybe you've worked with a gossipy person who loved to stir up trouble.

Don't despair. You're not alone. We've all been there. We've all had co-workers who brought chaos and dissension into the workplace and were every bit as destructive as the Four Horsemen of the Apocalypse. If we're honest, we'll admit that sometimes our own behavior added to the mess.

None of these situations are funny when we are struggling through them. They become funny in hindsight and when we realize we're not alone in our struggles against psycho bosses and obnoxious co-workers. So embrace the absurdity and see the funny side of it all.

The stories in this book originated in my weekly blog, HR Compliance Jungle. Some stories have a brief explanation of what inspired me. I could have added these comments as footnotes but I'm not an academic which means I'm not required to include footnotes. I've used sidebars instead in keeping with my lawyerly training. I've also included some of the wonderful feedback I've received from my loyal readers.

You'll notice that I haven't suggested how each situation should be resolved. Each story is followed by a short statement of what happened in the actual situation. I'll allow you to decide if you would have handled the problem the same way. That's because HR problems are usually fact-specific, even though there are employment laws that set the parameters for acceptable behavior. What works in one situation may not work in another. Employers need to assess what is reasonable in their specific situation.

I hope you'll enjoy reading this as much as I enjoyed writing it.

I - Psycho Bosses

Psycho Boss

The Lizard

> I was inspired to write this story because I had the distinction of working for two psycho bosses, both women. It was truly awful at the time but it's provided great material for my blog. Based on the reaction, I know many others also suffered from this type of workplace wacko.

Sue hates her job because she works for a psycho. Sue was transferred into the psycho's department during a company-wide reorganization about six months ago and life's gone steadily downhill since.

Sue's psycho boss loves to assign multiple projects with the same deadline, which pretty much guarantees that something won't be done on time. During the first month, Sue asked which project should be given priority and psycho boss always responded that the projects were equally important. So Sue stopped asking about prioritizing the workload. Of course, psycho boss blames Sue when deadlines are missed.

Refusing to establish priorities is just a symptom of psycho boss' standard management technique. Psycho boss refuses to make decisions because she's afraid to take responsibility. But she won't allow her subordinates to make any decisions without her input.

Last month, Sue decided to fight back. She bought a doll that she treats as her boss' avatar. Each evening, she sticks pins in the doll and wishes psycho boss would vanish. So far the doll looks like a pin cushion but the bad juju hasn't worked because Sue still works for the psycho.

Sue knows that senior management is aware of psycho boss' management deficiencies. But she also knows that they won't take any action as long as the work gets done and the grumbling doesn't flare into an open revolt. After all, senior management doesn't want to admit they made a mistake by promoting psycho boss in the first place.

Yesterday, psycho boss called Sue into her office to accuse Sue of incompetence. When Sue asked for specific examples based on her work, psycho boss started yelling and cursing, accusing Sue of insubordination. Now Sue is sitting at home, sticking pins in the doll and considering her options.

What are Sue's options?

1. She can take an advanced course in black magic and hope it works better than the juju doll.
2. She can complain to HR about psycho boss' unprofessional behavior (yelling and cursing) and request that an HR rep attend future meetings between Sue and psycho boss to serve as a witness.

3. She can look for another job either within the company or with another employer.

In the actual situation, the company reorganized departments again and psycho boss lost supervisory authority in the changes. So in a weird way the juju doll worked because psycho boss vanished.

You Want To Do What?

The Crow

Marcia is the HR manager for her company. She often feels that she's in a never-ending battle to balance management and employee expectations. Managers think employees lack loyalty to the company. Employees think the company doesn't care about them. Their most recent proof is the giant increase in employee contributions for health insurance.

Marcia endures almost daily requests from managers begging her to find ways to build employee morale and loyalty. Occasionally managers come up with their own morale-building ideas. Some of the kookiest ideas come from Roger, her least favorite manager.

Roger likes to search the internet for management techniques that he can implement with his subordinates. His bosses like his initiative because they aren't directly affected by his actions. Roger's bosses also don't see him every day and so are unaware of his general obnoxiousness.

Roger's subordinates, meanwhile, suffer through meetings where he drones on about the latest management theories while incessantly snapping his pen or drumming his fingers on the table, his coffee mug, or his chair arm. Roger also thinks he's invisible when making bodily adjustments, something his female subordinates find particularly gross and disgusting.

Roger's latest internet research leads him to 360° performance reviews. He reads the reviews about building team spirit and ignores the commentary cautioning that corporate culture can affect the outcome. The next day he marches into Marcia's office to demand 360° performance reviews for his people.

Marcia stares at Roger in blank amazement. He isn't obviously insane so she decides to give to him exactly what he's asked for. She can't resist chortling privately as she hands out the forms to each employee.

A couple of weeks later Marcia reads what Roger's employees have to say about him. As expected, they've vented their frustrations about his annoying personal habits and being treated as lab rats for his management theories. The reviews are so brutal she feels sorry for him. She invites Roger to her office for a private chat.

What should Marcia say to him?

1. She can soften the blow to Roger's ego by giving him an edited summary of what his employees think of him.
2. She can give him the unedited results and watch his ego deflate.

3. She can tell him that his brilliance is wasted at a branch location and encourage him to apply for a job at headquarters.

In the actual situation, the HR manager compiled the complaints she had received about Roger and presented this information to Roger's supervisor. The appalled senior manager was persuaded to reject 360º performance reviews before they were implemented. The old adage to "be careful what you wish for" applies to business as well as individuals. HR policies are most successful when they are carefully considered before being implemented.

I Don't Have a Drinking Problem

Lemmings

I changed some of the details but this one is based on a former workplace of mine. As social standards have evolved, employers have become less tolerant of alcoholism.

Leo and Ted are managers at their company. They were hired at the same time and became friends. They often ate lunch together and spent most afternoons at happy hour at their favorite sports bar.

Leo was promoted first. His division expanded rapidly and when he needed another manager, he asked for Ted. Ted managed the fastest growing product line in Leo's division. Naturally, Ted began thinking that his team should have a bigger budget. Leo said no. Ted went to happy hour alone to sulk.

In the next manager's meeting, Ted interrupted Leo repeatedly until Leo ordered him to shut up. After the meeting, Ted stomped into Leo's office to complain. Leo ordered Ted to leave and Ted refused. In the ensuing shoving match, two chairs were broken, Ted got a fat lip, and Leo had a bloody nose. After that, they went to separate bars for happy hour.

Ted decided to ask Leo's boss to make his team a separate division on the grounds that his team managed a product line worth more than all the rest of the products managed by Leo's division. Luckily for Ted, he'd made this appeal to Oscar.

Oscar is a fan of Star Trek and he runs a modified Klingon Empire, where you advance over the body of your former boss. He is happy to watch Leo and Ted scrap because if they are fighting each other they aren't challenging Oscar for his job. Oscar grants Ted's request.

Now Leo and Ted are trying to screw each other's careers by sucking up to Oscar. They suck up by inviting Oscar to happy hour. Oscar appreciates having Leo or Ted cover his bar tab. But all these soggy nights mean that productivity is suffering as Leo and Ted slide into alcoholism.

Nan, the HR manager, is watching from the sidelines. She knows she should talk to the senior management team about Leo's and Ted's potential disability due to alcoholism.

What options are available to Nan?

1. She can recommend that Leo and Ted be shipped off to rehab to dry out in hopes of saving their careers.
2. She can gather information about their poor performances to build a case for firing them.
3. She can wait to take action until a senior manager notices the problem.

In the actual case, each manager was encouraged to seek professional help for their alcoholism. Neither sought treatment. One manager eventually quit rather than be fired, while the other manager continued in his same role without any hope of a promotion.

Oscar continued working as a senior level manager and found other subordinates that he could pit against each other so that they would never threaten his position. Oscar was also an alcoholic who feared losing his position. To disguise his insecurities, he wavered between being an indecisive manager and a mercurial and unpredictable one.

I'm In Charge!

The Wolverine

A nanosecond after this blog appeared a loyal reader emailed me to ask if I had been reading the headlines in her city's newspaper. After a quick internet search, I realized that the scenario I described had unfolded in two cities simultaneously. What are the chances of that ever happening again?

Mary likes the arts and has volunteered for years with several non-profits. Recently, she was offered a paid part-time position. The pay is barely above minimum wage but includes a parking pass and it fits with her full-time job's schedule. Mary enjoys being paid to see the shows.

Mary's enthusiasm for her part-time arts job soon wears thin. Elaine is another part-timer who was recently promoted to manager to help supervise the part-time staff during peak attendance hours. Mary thinks the part-time managers are selected for their willingness to work longer hours for a small pay increase and not for their actual abilities.

Elaine is a perfect example. She bustles about acting important but has never been a manager. Under pressure, she becomes brusque to the point of rudeness. Since her main role is to resolve problems with unruly or disgruntled patrons, this creates interesting situations.

This evening, several patrons are shocked when their high-priced tickets to a special event are rejected. Elaine arrives as Mary is explaining that the ticket office can help sort out their ticketing problem. Mary explains to Elaine that the tickets are not scanning properly.

Elaine examines the tickets and tells the patrons that buying from scalpers is never a good idea. One patron turns red with fury as he says the third party ticketing company he used is a recognized distributor for the non-profit. Mary offers to show the patrons to the ticketing office but Elaine orders her to stay at her post. Elaine stalks off.

Twenty minutes later, Elaine is back. In front of other workers, she tells Mary to never leave her post again. Mary points out that she didn't. Then Elaine accuses Mary of "throwing gasoline on a fire" by telling the angry patrons that the ticket office could fix the ticketing problems. Elaine claims that the patrons will think this guarantees them admittance to the sold-out show. Mary's temper rises.

What are Mary's options?

1. She can complain to Elaine's boss but he is unlikely to take action unless other employees have also complained about Elaine.

2. She can suggest that Elaine take Prozac or learn yoga to deal with the stress of being in charge.
3. She can accept that Elaine's accusations arise from feeling insecure and brush them off unless Elaine continues to criticize her.

In the actual situation, Mary resigned from the part-time job a few weeks later saying that she was too busy to continue working at the non-profit. She never complained to the HR Department because she believed they would do nothing about the abusive co-worker.

Non-profits face the same employee issues as for-profit companies but often mistakenly believe they are exempt from employment laws. As a general rule, they are not and should consider how best to minimize their risks of violating employment laws.

How Did I Get Into This Mess?

The Cape Buffalo

> Another true story from one of my former employers. I found out about this unique method for funding "employee appreciation" because I was the corporate lawyer advising the HR department and one of them let it slip during a routine conversation.

Veronica has been feeling a bit down lately as she drives to work. As the HR manager for her company, she's in charge of the plans for the company's annual employee picnic. She tried delegating this responsibility but gave up when the employees she asked threatened to quit rather than get stuck with the job.

Veronica understands why they refused to help. The company picnic is not fun. Younger employees think pie eating contests are disgusting and they don't care about activities for kids because they don't have children. Alcohol was banned two years ago (for reasons that can't be discussed because the lawyers are still sorting out liability for the "proximate cause" of certain alleged injuries). Older workers are simply disenchanted and the ones with marketable skills are bailing out as fast as they can update their resumes.

Veronica understands that, too. She tried for years to bridge the gap between the employees and the company owners. The owners refer to their employees as "talent" when talking to investors and other outsiders but they treat their workers like talentless twits. They micromanage all aspects of the workplace and have a well-developed snitch system for obtaining reports on "disloyalty". The owners disguise their apparent contempt for their employees by insisting on annual gruesome rituals like the company picnic.

Unfortunately, this year a possible riot is brewing. Employees recently learned that the company gets a cut of the money collected from the vending machines in the break room. The owners have been using that money to cover the costs of the company picnic, meaning the employees are paying for their own company picnic.

What are Sue's options?

1. She can meet with the company owners to explain the mood of employees and ask them to cancel the picnic or to approve a budget to do something special this year.
2. She can do the minimum necessary to stage the picnic and expect that even fewer employees will show up than did last year.
3. She can polish up her resume and discreetly market her services to other companies with better employment practices.

In the actual situation, about half the employees called in sick or used vacation days to avoid attending the picnic. The oblivious and tone-deaf company owners complained that the employees were disloyal ingrates.

I've Had It With You!

The Warthog

This is a sanitized version of an actual supervisor-subordinate relationship at one of my former employers. No one lived happily ever after.

Once there was an executive assistant (what we used to call a secretary) who worked for a toxic boss. Rachel was an average performer capable of doing her job but you'd never know it from David. Rachel and David joined the company a few months apart more than ten years ago. They only began working together about two years ago.

Before that, Rachel worked for several managers who gave her neutral or mildly positive marks on her annual performance review. The unexciting performance reviews kept Rachel on the move, transferring to new managers in hopes of finding a better work relationship. Now Rachel is desperate to move again because she's had it with David.

David is mean and nasty. He criticizes her work product mercilessly, often when other people are present. He makes snarky comments about her constant noshing even though Rachel has explained that she has a medical condition requiring her to eat healthy snacks frequently throughout the day.

David's nastiness stems, at least in part, from Rachel's mediocre performance. He's had it with her, too. He'll never admit that his constant disapproval has affected her performance. After all, he also answers to a difficult boss and doesn't want to hear any whining from others. He'd love to offload Rachel on another manager but there haven't been any openings.

Last week, David's and Rachel's luck changed when an internal job posting announced an opening for an executive assistant in another department. Rachel immediately submits her resume. The HR manager tells Rachel that she's not eligible for consideration because David still needs to submit her performance review.

Rachel dashes out of the HR manager's office and makes it to David's office in Olympic gold-medal time. She glares at David and demands that he turn in her performance review immediately. David scowls at her. Then he says that he will give her the best damned review she's ever had if it means he can get rid of her.

What can Rachel do next?
1. She can complain to HR about David's abusive attitude but that could make her sound whiny and hurt her chances of a transfer away from him.
2. She can dump her trash of rotting apple cores on his desk when he's in a meeting.

3. She can say nothing and use his "great" review to get away from him.

In the actual situation, the executive assistant moved from one toxic manager to an even more toxic manager. The HR department was unable to tackle the toxic managers due to the organization's internal politics which rewarded seniority and personal friendships rather than competence or emotional maturity. Even the best HR policies can't fix some things.

Masters of The Universe

Peacocks

> If you're a survivor of the downsizing, rightsizing, and reengineering of the 1980's corporate world you'll probably experience PTSD just reading this one. For those who weren't there, a quick internet search of "Chainsaw Al" will reveal one of the most notorious examples of that era.

Jim and Tony run a venture capital fund that specializes in distressed assets. They buy companies, replace the management team, cut most of the employees to generate savings and make the company look profitable (on paper). Then they sell the company.

A business magazine features them in an article and uses the term "Masters of the Universe". After the feature article, Jim and Tony decide to branch out from distressed assets and buy a company that has been successful without being spectacular.

Jim and Tony begin their ownership by holding a company-wide meeting with employees at which they talk about the company's wonderful financial future. Linda interrupts this sales pitch by asking them to reconcile these comments with their established practice of boosting profits by firing most workers. Jim evades her question. So Larry asks point blank how many jobs will be cut. Jim looks at Tony. Tony shrugs. The meeting ends abruptly.

After studying the company's bottom line, Jim and Tony decide that the first employees to go are Linda and Larry. They tell Sandra, the HR rep, to prepare the paperwork. She cautions against firing two of the most respected workers. Jim looks at the org chart again and concludes they are peons.

On Friday, Linda and Larry are ushered out the door. Their first port of call is an employment law attorney where they discuss wrongful termination, retaliation, and age discrimination. The attorney has a vision of becoming famous by taking down the Masters of the Universe. He agrees to represent Linda and Larry.

Within weeks, a third of the workforce resigns following Linda and Larry out the door. Jim and Tony are initially relieved; they only had to fire two workers. But the remaining workforce is demoralized. Within six months, the company has lost several key clients and the bottom line is tanking. Jim and Tony call a meeting with Sandra to discuss staffing levels and the status of Linda's and Larry's lawsuit.

What should Sandra tell them?

1. She can say that she warned them that firing Linda and Larry would have dire consequences.
2. She can tell them that as Masters of The Universe, she expects them to solve their own problems.

3. She can hand in her resignation, having already received several job offers.

The above scenario is a slightly exaggerated version of the actual events following a corporate acquisition. The new owners were so focused on the numbers they saw employees as a bottom line cost rather than as vital contributors to the company's success. In a corporate merger or acquisition, it's critically important to create a plan with HR for handling inevitable layoffs in order to smooth the transition.

Working With a Jerk

The Weasel

Another true story, with some details changed, that I lived through. I didn't like the job but I'm now grateful for the professional knowledge and skills I gained during my time with these guys.

Jenny is excited about her new job with an insurance company. She isn't excited about insurance, of course; no one is. She's excited about being employed again. None of her previous jobs lasted very long as her employers were acquired or downsized.

Jenny's new boss, Ed, assigns her to work with a more experienced co-worker, Alan. Jenny trots down the hall to Alan's office to introduce herself. Alan's office is a mess with files stacked haphazardly on the desk and floor. It looks like a fire marshal's exhibit of a fire hazard.

Jenny says that Ed has asked her to work with Alan while she is in training. She asks how she can help him with some of the claims he is working on. Alan flips through several folders on his messy desk and says he'll get back to her.

After a week of stalling, Alan agrees to take Jenny along to a meeting with an insured that has filed a claim. The insured company's office is on the other side of town. During the meeting, Alan tells Jenny to wait while he goes down the hall to look at some sensitive documents. Jenny waits in the conference room talking to a representative of the insured.

Finally, she asks whether Alan has finished his review of the sensitive documents. She learns that he left twenty minutes ago. Jenny is stranded at the insured's office late in the day as rush hour begins. She calls a cab to take her back to her office where she parked her car.

The next day Jenny tells Ed that she would like to work with a different co-worker. She doesn't tell Ed all the details of the prior day's meeting but says that the current arrangement isn't working. Ed calls Alan to his office and asks how things are going with Jenny's training. Alan acts surprised and says he thinks it's going well.

What should Jenny do next?

1. She can tell Ed what really happened but she's the new kid on the block and there's no guarantee he'll believe her.
2. She can complain to the HR representative who is 800 miles away at the company HQ and has a history of deferring to local managers.
3. She can bide her time learning as much as possible so that she can find a better job with nicer co-workers.

In the actual situation, Jenny chose the third option. She learned new skills that increased her marketability and eventually moved to a new employer with nicer co-workers.

Mentor, Schmentor

The Hyena

> This story was inspired by a friend of mine who worked at a law firm where this happened. A female partner won a bucketful of service awards for her mentorship of young female attorneys. The problem? Her female subordinates said none of them had ever been mentored by her. But the firm was happy because they could brag about their diversity & inclusion program and their policy of mentoring young lawyers.
> Moral of the story: Talk to the lower level folks about the real workplace culture before joining a particular employer.

Grace is an assistant manager for her company. She's always looking for opportunities to improve her performance so she can get promoted. She hears that Diane believes in mentoring young talent and asks for a transfer to Diane's department.

At their first meeting, they set performance goals for Grace. Grace wants to take some management classes to prepare for promotion. She also wants more responsibility to prove that she can be a good manager.

Diane applauds her goals and immediately asks Grace to help train a new hire, David. Diane also encourages Grace to be "proactive" by volunteering for internal assignments as part of a strategy to get noticed by senior management.

So Grace volunteers to lead a team that will make recommendations for streamlining some of the company's operating procedures. Diane forwards the committee's recommendations to senior management. A month later, Grace reads an email from the company president that praises Diane for the committee's recommendations.

Grace asks Diane why none of the committee members were mentioned in the president's email and receives an evasive answer. Grace concludes that she and her team will never be recognized. She decides to do all she can to help her committee members get recognized for their hard work. She's already quietly mentoring three of them and helps two of them find places in departments away from Diane.

She decides to not bail out herself because she believes she is in line for a promotion that is opening soon. The company has a policy that requires an employee to be in a position for at least a year before being eligible for promotion.

This morning Grace learns that David will get the promotion she wanted. She also learns that the company is supporting Diane's nomination for an award based on her mentorship of younger women professionals. Grace asks several female co-workers; no one knows who Diane is supposed to have mentored.

What should Grace do next?

1. She can create a fake resume for David and send it to competitors in the hopes they will hire him, leaving her the promotion she deserves.
2. She can accept that Diane's nickname starts with a capital "B" and stop volunteering to do work for which Diane will steal the credit.
3. She can recognize that her career advancement requires an internal transfer or a new employer.

The above scenario is a composite of the experiences of many women, and some men, professionals. Managers like Diane can tank morale faster than obviously rotten managers. A good HR program should include performance assessments that neutralize the toxic effect of a Diane. Of course, as noted above, HR policies can't fix a workplace where Diane is rewarded by her supervisors for fulfilling a corporate goal ("she checks all the right boxes") without regard to the collateral damage done to her subordinates.

My Boss Hates Me!

The Rhino

> A kernel of truth can mutate into assumptions and perceptions that poison the workplace. This story arose from a dispute I witnessed years ago. I'm betting most of you have seen these scenarios first-hand, too.

Teresa works at a major corporation and she's grown steadily more pessimistic about her job and career. She's convinced that her boss, Barbara, has discriminated against her and she complains to HR. Her discrimination complaint is investigated by Audrey, the HR rep.

Audrey invites Teresa to a confidential meeting to get her side of the story. Teresa shows up at the meeting toting a giant 3-ring binder stuffed full of copies of emails between Teresa and Barbara and copies of performance appraisals. Teresa says the binder contains proof that Barbara is out to get her.

Audrey has an awful sinking feeling, familiar to any experienced

HR person, as she stares at the 3-ring binder. She will eventually have to read it as part of her investigation. She sighs heavily and delays the inevitable by continuing her interview of Teresa.

Teresa spins a tale of slights, oversights, and harsh words that she says add up to discrimination. She claims that Barbara cuts her off in mid-sentence every time she tries to talk during staff meetings. Barbara is rude to her and makes negative comments in front of co-workers. Barbara gives pay raises to younger, less experienced co-workers while telling Teresa that she's not eligible for any pay increases. Barbara ignores her and dislikes her while being nice to everyone else in the department.

The next day, Audrey begins reading the 3-ring binder. After an hour, she has a raging headache but has reached a few conclusions. The emails indicate that Teresa has become increasingly defensive, responding to sometimes non-existent criticism. The performance appraisals completed by Barbara move from neutral ("works well with others") assessments to mildly negative ("attitude needs improvement") in the most recent appraisal.

Audrey knows that Barbara has a history of managerial issues. Audrey had opposed Barbara's promotion to manager because of her lack of "people" skills. Now Audrey is sitting at her desk trying to decide what to do next.

What should Audrey do?

1. She can recommend that nothing be done due to a lack of clear proof of discrimination.
2. She can arrange Teresa's transfer to a different manager and

hope for the best.

3. She can tell Teresa and Barbara to stop acting like whiny children and then go have a glass (or a bottle) of wine to wash away the effects of their feud.

In the actual situation, a department reorganization lead to the reassignment of the disgruntled employee. That resolved the immediate conflict but not the long term issue of poor training for new managers.

Promoted To Failure

The Wasp

> This is another true story from one of my former employers, which has been slightly fictionalized for the protection of all. I sat on the sidelines and watched the show unfold. I was shocked by the outcome until I learned to embrace the absurdity of it all.

Julia, the HR manager, is watching her company's diversity and inclusion program go hideously wrong. Julia pushed every level of management all the way to the C-suite, urging them to broaden the pool of employees eligible for promotion to management. What did all her effort get her? Margaret.

Margaret worked in operations for many years and understands the technical side of the job but her interpersonal skills are dismal. She's whiny and needy and self-absorbed. Some of her shortcomings might have been fixed if the C-suite had accepted Julia's recommendation to create a management training program.

Instead, Margaret was promoted to manager without training or a mentor to help her. Now she micromanages her subordinates and refuses to delegate any decision-making authority to them. But she's afraid of being held responsible if something goes wrong so she fails to make any decisions.

When other department managers complain that their work is disrupted, Margaret accuses her subordinates of incompetence. Her subordinates show up and don't do their jobs since they know Margaret is likely to undermine any actions they take. Most of them are applying for transfers away from her.

The stress on Margaret is so intense that she suffers from migraines and works from home several days a week. When she does come into the office, she is so unpleasant that everyone avoids her.

The steady rumble of discontent is growing so loud that the C-suite is having trouble ignoring it. Julia is desperately searching for a solution to the whole mess but she's run out of time. In today's mail she receives an EEOC notice letter that Margaret's secretary has made a complaint of racial discrimination against Margaret.

What should Julia do next?

1. She can recommend that Margaret be appointed special liaison to the company's suppliers with an immediate posting to, say, Shanghai or Taipei.
2. She can investigate the charges and then artfully respond to the EEOC in a way that is slightly more flattering than the actual situation warrants.
3. She can notify the C-Suite of the EEOC investigation and

use this as an opportunity to convince the senior managers to approve a training program for new managers.

In the actual situation, the EEOC concluded there was no racial discrimination because Margaret treated all her subordinates like crap. The employer hailed this decision as a victory. Margaret was eventually reassigned during a departmental reorganization but the employer still doesn't have a training program for new managers.

Let Me Do It!

The Magpie

> Another true story from my checkered work history. This supervisor was actually a pretty nice guy but he couldn't stop meddling in the details.

Sarah joined the company as an experienced lateral hire. She was attracted to the company after they offered her a chance to use her diverse experience. Sarah likes variety because she's easily bored by routine. She bailed out of several previous jobs when they became boring. Now she does all the special projects for her new employer and each day offers a new challenge. She likes everything about her job except her boss, Dean.

Dean is the second most dreaded type of boss: the micromanager. Dean can't just assign a project to Sarah. He spends half an hour explaining in detail how he would complete the project. Then he tells Sarah to use her own judgment.

Sarah has high personal standards that require her to thoroughly research an issue before making recommendations. She is also a perfectionist who agonizes over each memo and report to ensure that the information is accurate and the words are clear and concise. Then Dean ruins it.

As her boss, Dean wants to see Sarah's written memos and reports before they are sent on to the senior management team. Sarah understands the need for quality control but he's a micromanager and he can't resist meddling. His review of her first report for the higher ups resulted in a sea of red ink. Dean had revised the entire report.

Sarah stared at her destroyed sentences and asked Dean why he had changed them. He said he thought the report read better with the changes. Sarah pointed out that all the changes were stylistic. Essentially, he had re-written her report to reflect his more verbose style of writing. Dean smiled and assured Sarah that things would change as he became familiar with the quality of her work.

Of course, nothing changes. As the months pass, Sarah's frustration grows. She daydreams of beating Dean senseless with his own laptop computer or forcing him to listen to rap music. She discreetly asks the HR director to transfer her to a different manager but is told such a move is impossible.

What options are available to Sarah?

1. She can continue hoping that Dean's management style will change.
2. She can continue objecting to Dean's management style, which is contributing to a perception that she's bitchy and

not a team player.

3. She can do the minimum necessary to earn her paycheck while she looks for another employer.

In the actual situation, the subordinate eventually found a new employer where her new boss assigned projects, noted the deadline, and then stepped away unless his assistance was requested.

The Peter Principle Strikes Again

The Sheep

Yes, it's based on yet another true story from one of my former employers. This supervisor was a nice guy but was hopelessly clueless. Fortunately, he was also a good sport when teased about his cluelessness.

Edith is the HR manager for her company and she usually likes her job. Each day is different as co-workers find new and inventive ways to get themselves into difficulties. Edith has a double espresso each morning to fortify herself for the latest adventures.

But Edith's toughest employee situation doesn't involve the usual employee misadventures. It involves Bruce, one of the division managers. Bruce is a nice, inoffensive guy who is liked by everyone who doesn't work for him. He is also destroying his division.

Bruce's career started promisingly enough. He graduated from college with honors and immediately was hired by the company.

He's technically proficient and his attention to detail is legendary. In fact, he often gets so wrapped up in the details that he forgets about deadlines.

A year ago, Bruce's bosses several levels up the chain of command were looking for someone who could be counted on to do the work but to never threaten their position in the company. They ignored Bruce's immediate supervisor who pointed out that Bruce has fewer social skills than a person reared by wolves. Bruce was promoted.

The damage was obvious immediately to anyone paying attention. In his first staff meeting, Bruce enthusiastically talked about a magazine article he'd read that described how blue whales communicate. His subordinates sat listening in stunned disbelief. After all, the purpose of the meeting was to discuss new sales metrics for their division.

It turns out Bruce's first staff meeting was a high point on the road to destruction. The cleverest and most marketable employees are bailing out to join competitors. One woman is so affected by her experiences that she is now a novice Buddhist nun in Nepal.

Edith struggles to contain the damage caused by Bruce's incredibly inept leadership. She's convinced that Bruce is aware of his shortcomings as a leader but he won't admit it. She asks for a meeting with senior management.

What should Edith tell the senior managers?

1. She can provide examples of Bruce's ineffective leadership and suggest that he be replaced by someone with better "people" skills.

2. She can request management training for Bruce to help him improve his leadership skills.
3. She can demand a pay raise and a bigger budget to hire replacements for the employees chased off by Bruce's lousy management skills.

In the actual situation, senior management remained happy with the ineffective manager. He kept his job until he was undermined and then replaced by his most ambitious subordinate. He happily continued to work and was deeply relieved to no longer have supervisory responsibilities.

Act Your Age!

The Tasmanian Devil

> This story is based on a client's messy situation. It came to light during my interviews with other employees on an entirely different set of problems. The HR manager was new to her role and unsure of the scope of her authority; but even a battle-hardened HR manager would have struggled to sort out these folks.

Jerry feels besieged and overloaded. He's the CEO and he ought to be bragging about his business. Instead he's hiding in his office while he decides what to do next.

It all started a couple of months ago when two supervisors had a misunderstanding. Brown-nosing Bette and motor-mouth Mike each thought the other was responsible for losing a key customer. Their last face-to-face meeting degenerated into a yelling, name-calling mess where coffee cups were hurled across the table and a cheese Danish was smashed into the face of Bette's assistant. Now they communicate strictly by email.

Since they're supervisors, they've managed to drag their respective subordinates into the fight. Soon everyone is communicating via emails that are full of adjectives more appropriate to the schoolyard or a political campaign. Their subordinates don't even use the same bathrooms anymore to avoid talking face-to-face.

Jerry doesn't notice any of the fighting. He's busy talking to investors that he needs to finance a new product. Besides, he's the CEO and people talk differently to him. His first inkling that all is not well is when several customers switch to competitors rather than renewing their contracts.

Jerry asks brown-nosing Bette why the heck her team of salespeople let the customers get away. She blames motor-mouth Mike's technical team for not answering questions about the products, which meant her team couldn't answer customer questions. Jerry asks Mike what's going on and he blames Bette's team of dunces.

Jerry asks the HR manager, Liz, if she's heard any complaints from co-workers about Bette and Mike. Liz admits she has. Jerry asks why the heck she didn't tell him. Liz is hurt; she's doing her best.

Liz shows him a series of email exchanges and that's when Jerry learns the awful truth about Bette and Mike. He can feel the top of his skull popping off as his blood pressure rises. Now he's sitting in his office trying to decide what to do.

What options are available to Jerry?

1. He can fire Bette and Mike for showing the emotional development of pre-teens.
2. He can empty the corporate bank account and "retire" to the

Cayman Islands to drink rum.

3. He can counsel Bette and Mike to act like grownups and work together for the company.

In the actual situation, the employer chose the third option. The employer's decision was based on an assessment of the supervisors' capabilities and skills. The employer also needed to follow the company's progressive discipline policy before firing employees.

What'd You Say?

The Guinea Pig

> This story was inspired by two experiences I had. In the first, I had a manager whose utterances often sounded like gibberish. The second was a solemn occasion when I struggled not to guffaw because the keynote speaker lisped like Sylvester, the cat in the Bugs Bunny cartoons. What if these experiences happened simultaneously in the workplace, I wondered......

Bob has been a manager for a long time but his department has a lot of turnover because more experienced employees refuse to work for him. Ann is a new hire who thinks he's a lot nicer than the jerk she used to work for. But after a week of working for Bob, she begins to understand why no one wants to work for him.

On her first day, Bob tells her to feed the field porcupine. Ann stares blankly at him and asks him to repeat his instructions. Bob frowns and tells her again to feed the field porcupine. Ann slips out of his office and flags down a co-worker. Eventually they figure out that he wants Ann to find the paper file for a client named Field.

On another occasion, he tells Ann to call Dodd Maxson. She searches the customer records but can't find Dodd Maxson. Luckily a co-worker recalls a large client account that Bob's working on and suggests looking for a guy named Rod Waxman. Ann wonders what he'll say next.

Soon after the Waxman mix up, he tells her to talk to the three bears about an appointment he needs with the CEO. Ann figures out with assistance that Bob wants her to talk to Patrice Burns, the CEO's executive assistant. By now Ann thinks she's catching on.

When Bob tells her to talk to the care box about the cost of dipping snuff, she uses her old charades skills to think of rhyming words that might match what Bob said. Bob is going to a sales convention out of town and he mentioned something about shipping his marketing materials. She cleverly concludes that Bob wants her to ask the warehouse what it would cost to ship his stuff to the trade show.

Now Ann is sitting in the office of Sarah, the HR rep, who asks how she's settling in to her new job. Ann says guardedly that there are challenges but overall it's going well. Then Sarah asks how it's going with Bob.

What should Ann say?

1. She can say that Bob is an anthropology project who is creating his own language and testing it on unsuspecting subordinates.
2. She can lie and say everything is wonderful and hope that her increased consumption of red wine each evening will help

her to eventually understand Bob.

3. She can remember that she's the new kid on the block and maintain a neutral attitude.

In the actual situation, the employees good-naturedly poked fun at their manager's garbled instructions. Eventually the manager learned to speak more clearly and his subordinates learned to repeat his instructions to ensure they heard correctly.

II

Obnoxious Co-Workers

Why Was I So Nice To The Punk?

The Rattlesnake

> Apparently everyone has worked with a Mercedes because I received plenty of feedback. Here's my favorite email response: "I hate Mercedes too. Let's do lunch."

Janice feels old and unappreciated. She does her job quietly with little fuss and needs minimal supervision because she's seen and done it all before. In fact, she manages everything so smoothly that she rarely draws attention.

Janice didn't mind the lack of acknowledgement for her contributions until a few months ago. That's when her work space was invaded by a much younger worker, Mercedes. Mercedes is friendly with a hint of insecurity because she's learning to do tasks she's never done before.

Janice remembers joining a new company and being "trained" by an old bat who deliberately omitted key information in the hopes that Janice would fail. So Janice is happy to pass along tips, hints, and advice to help Mercedes learn her job.

But Mercedes is ambitious and her insecurities leave her craving public affirmation of her contributions. She sees everyone, especially Janice, as a threat. She begins copying their boss on nitpicky emails asking Janice for information rather than simply asking her. They sit less than five feet apart.

Janice doesn't say anything because she doesn't want to sound like a whiner but she's rapidly reaching the conclusion that Mercedes is the Wicked Witch of The South. Janice daydreams of teaching Mercedes a real lesson in bureaucratic backstabbing. It all remains a fantasy until today's staff meeting.

Mercedes is reporting at the staff meeting about a project she inherited from Janice. She drags out her report with lots of "ums" and "uhs" explaining how she revised the metrics and pulled together all the information. Never once does she acknowledge her debt to Janice who created the whole thing so that Mercedes only had to collate information and do some data entry.

Janice looks at their boss who is smiling at Mercedes like a proud mom watching her clever child successfully finish the school recital. Janice feels the top of her skull evaporating in a mushroom cloud as Mercedes is praised.

What options are available to Janice?

1. She can spike Mercedes' protein shake with a laxative before the next staff meeting.
2. She can create a fake resume showing Mercedes as the most brilliant person since Einstein and mass mail it to every recruiter in the country.

3. She can recognize that Mercedes is immature and let someone else kick the stuffing out of her (figuratively speaking, of course).

In the actual situation, Janice remembered some of her gaffes as a young professional and chose to not retaliate against Mercedes. Sometimes managers are so focused on coaching younger workers for success they forget to acknowledge the contributions of older workers. Building a team means recognizing the contributions of all team members. In Janice's case, the manager acknowledged that she had focused on Mercedes but was cognizant of Janice's contributions to the team.

Sharing Sharon

The Chicken

After she read this blog, one reader approached me at a networking event to tell me about her office's Sharon.

Sharon is a middling performer, not great but not so bad that her job's on the chopping block. She's willing to work with any team to which she is assigned and she can be depended on to slog through some of the more tedious work.

Unfortunately for her co-workers, Sharon believes in sharing the details of her life. Her co-workers call her "Sharing Sharon," as well as a few other names not fit to print here. Sharon's co-workers know all about her marital problems, her son's attention deficit disorder, and her teenaged daughter's complicated love life. They also know about her cat's litterbox problems and suffered for a week while Sharon agonized over her decision to put down her aging, sick dog.

Sharon cares about more than just her family, of course. One week she insists people should do more to save furry baby animals before all non-human species become extinct. Another week she explains that she's reducing her carbon imprint by avoiding plastic water bottles.

Sharing Sharon's oversharing is beginning to affect operations. One worker twisted her ankle when several employees imitated the running of the bulls to clear the break room to avoid Sharon. Several co-workers told the HR manager, Pam, that they would rather quit the company, losing their 401(k) match, than be stuck on another team with Sharon.

Pam has tried several times to give Sharon a hint that her personal life is better shared on Facebook with personal friends than with co-workers. Sharon just doesn't get it. The breaking point Pam feared has now happened. Sharon was busy oversharing in a team meeting and the team leader was finally goaded beyond endurance. He yelled at Sharon to "shut up, already"!

Now Sharon is sitting in Pam's office, sobbing and begging for Pam's help.

How should Pam handle this situation?

1. She can privately thank the team leader with a bottle of Gentleman Jack for saying what all of Sharon's co-workers wanted to say but were afraid to.
2. She can sympathize with Sharon's distress but remind her (again) that personal lives shouldn't be brought into the workplace.
3. She can counsel the team leader regarding the company's anti-bullying policy which prohibits derogatory comments

to co-workers, sympathize with his exhausted patience, and encourage him to find less brutal ways to make his point in future.

In the actual situation, the co-workers continued to cringe and hide until their Sharing Sharon accepted a job at a competitor.

Go Back To Your Cave

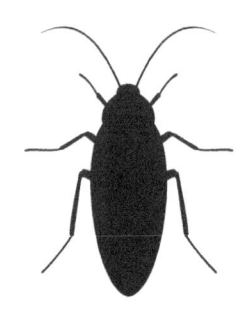

The Cockroach

> Every workplace has at least one troglodyte. They can be male or female. This troglodyte is a composite of a couple that I worked with over the years.

Once upon a time, at a company not so different from its competitors, a new employee was hired. Trudy was bright, cheerful, and had graduated from college near the top of her class. She believed that hard work was all she needed to advance her career.

As with every fairytale, an evil troglodyte lurked in a cubicle down the hall. His name was Larry. He joined the company many years ago and never advanced beyond cubicle world. Beneath a façade of pleasant chitchat lurks a very angry employee.

Trudy bumps into Larry in the break room as she tries to figure out how to use the single cup coffee maker. Larry helps her while sarcastically commenting about how good life was when they still had the Mr. Coffee machine. Trudy finds his acidic commentary mildly amusing and thinks he might be a friend.

Alas for the fair maid. At the next staff meeting, Larry questions the decision of Jennifer, the manager, to designate Trudy as the leader on a new project. Larry privately thinks he should be leading the team based on his seniority. Trudy seals her fate by saying she'd be happy to have his help. Jennifer shrugs and agrees. She's a manager, not a knight in shining armor trying to rescue a fair maid, especially one too stupid to sniff out danger.

Trudy's first hint that she is not going to live happily ever after happens at her first team meeting. Larry interrupts repeatedly with helpful suggestions, all of which she rejects. During the next week, Larry visits each team member to express his concerns about the imminent failure of the project due to Trudy's inexperience.

Jennifer hears via the grapevine that the project is tanking so she calls Trudy in for a status report. Larry sees Trudy walking down the hallway towards Jennifer's office. Quick as a flash he scampers down the hallway, pushes past her and turns in the doorway to Jennifer's office to smirk before slamming the door in Trudy's face.

When Trudy finally meets with Jennifer, Larry's poisonous comments have taken effect. Jennifer dislikes Larry but she's been having second thoughts about assigning an important project to such a young subordinate. Jennifer says she's worried about progress and needs to replace Trudy with an older, more experienced worker.

What should Trudy do next?

1. She can loudly proclaim that Larry the troglodyte has

sabotaged her career and begin crying.
2. She can plot a suitable revenge against Larry but he's had years more experience at this sort of backstabbing.
3. She can search for a mentor to help her learn how to fight troglodytes in the future.

In the actual situation, the new employee gave up believing in fairytales, resigned and joined a competitor, feeling older and slightly wiser. Avoid this fairytale by implementing effective HR policies, such as creating a mentorship program to help employees develop the soft skills needed for success.

Chaos Cathy

The Rat

> Moral of the story: Nobody likes a whiner. But whiners may also be a symptom of deeper HR problems, much like the canary in the coal mine. This story was inspired by a former workplace that had many HR issues caused by senior management's attitude toward employees. One employee chose to whine about the things she could not change.

Chaos Cathy is a good worker when she pays attention to her job. Too bad she spends most of her time picking fights with her co-workers. One week she complains about a co-worker's perfume. Another week she complains about loud voices talking on the phone.

Chaos Cathy's whining is a symptom of her perpetual competitiveness. She complains that her cubicle is smaller than the cubicles of her peers. After weeks of drama, her manager finally agrees to find another cubicle. But the new cubicle has no window. So Chaos Cathy is still unhappy, even though the window in the old smaller cubicle offers only a view of the trash bins behind the building.

Chaos Cathy's boss flatly refuses to move Rob, a more senior worker, from his cubicle so that Cathy can have it. Chaos Cathy flounces down the stairs to Weary Wanda, the HR manager, to complain that offering a windowless cubicle is retaliation for complaining about the terrible working conditions. Wanda is weary because she's got to listen to Chaos Cathy's constant whining while also getting an earful from Cathy's annoyed co-workers.

Weary Wanda is an experienced HR manager and mom. She lets Chaos Cathy rant while her mind drifts to what she'd like to eat for dinner that night. Eventually Chaos Cathy stops talking. Weary Wanda says she'll look into the matter and encourages Chaos Cathy to go back to work.

A week later, Chaos Cathy is back. Now she's complaining that her manager has encouraged his other subordinates to abuse her for exposing his incompetence. Chaos Cathy launches into a convoluted description of abusive co-workers, travel to Mars, and stinky perfume from the next cubicle to prove her boss is incompetent and prejudiced.

Weary Wanda asks how Chaos Cathy would like to have her complaints resolved. Cathy replies that she wants her manager to get off the planet. Weary Wanda explains that HR can't force a supervisor to get off the planet so Chaos Cathy needs to think of another solution to the problem. Chaos Cathy says no other outcome is acceptable to her.

What are Weary Wanda's options?

1. She can recommend that Chaos Cathy drink more boxed red wine in the evenings to calm her nerves.

2. She can transfer Chaos Cathy to another department run by a supervisor that Wanda doesn't like.
3. She can explain, as politely as possible, that chronic complainers like Chaos Cathy rarely help their long-term career aspirations.

In the actual situation, the complaining employee's insubordinate behavior towards her manager escalated until her employment was terminated. She unsuccessfully sued for wrongful termination.

The Knife In The Back

The Cobra

> Yes, I worked in a place where the executive assistant actually stood near the elevators to keep tabs on attendance, which she promptly reported to the owner of the company. So I started taking the stairs, which foiled her and improved my lung capacity.

Bryan is a serial entrepreneur. Every time he gets a new idea, he starts a new company to exploit the idea. He's successful at starting businesses but he's lousy at running them.

Bryan doesn't like getting bogged down in the details. So he relies on lieutenants to keep him informed of how things are going at each company. Unfortunately, Bryan doesn't seem to have noticed that one of his trusted lieutenants is deadlier than a rattlesnake.

Gail learns this when she begins working at one of his companies. Her first day on the job, she's introduced to Pam who is so friendly and helpful that Gail is duped into thinking she's nice. But Pam is a snake in the grass.

Pam is an intolerable busybody. She stands near the elevator to track the time each employee shows up for work. She wanders the hallways keeping tabs on what others are doing and saying. Then she passes every tidbit of information along to Bryan with a special Pam twist.

Gail learns the truth when Bryan stops by for a quarterly meeting with the company's management team, of which Gail is a junior member. Bryan marches into the conference room and sits opposite Pam who is taking notes on the decisions he makes.

Bryan begins the meeting by chewing out Laura for falling sales in the past quarter. Laura replies that it is impossible to boost sales when her team is starved for resources. She produces a stack of receipts showing that her team has to buy their own office supplies since Pam locked up the supply closet and hid the key.

Bryan impatiently tells Laura to stop blaming others for her own failings as a manager. Then he turns on Bob, the CFO, who didn't have the financial reports ready for Bryan. Bob scowls but says nothing.

Gail knows that Bob was late with the financial reports because Pam delayed working on them while she worked on other lower priority assignments. Gail looks at Pam expecting her to defend Bob. Pam smirks and remains silent.

What are Gail's options?

1. She can point out that Pam sabotaged Bob, though Bryan probably won't believe her.

2. She can thank her lucky stars that Pam isn't gunning for her.
3. She can use her accrued vacation to begin hunting for a new job, preferably one without another Pam.

In the actual situation, the junior manager soon found herself on the backstabber's hit list and left the company as soon as possible.

Queen Bee

The Bee

This story evolved from the saga of a training session that I taught with a colleague. She spotted "Adelaide's" behavior during my presentation and I confirmed it during her part of the dog and pony show. It was a surreal day in the boonies of east Tennessee.

Adam is a branch manager for his company and he's coasting toward retirement. He lost interest in his current career long ago after several major battles with his assistant. Her name is Adelaide and officially she's the executive assistant but unofficially she's been running the branch office since Jimmy Carter's administration.

When Adelaide decides how things should be done, everyone agrees. If they don't, their careers take a nosedive as Adam learned during his first year as branch manager. He came in full of ideas for improving efficiency but Adelaide decided the office was fine "as is." After months of battling she won and Adam began planning his post-retirement career.

Adam's boss isn't happy and he's trying to figure out how to increase profits in Adam's office. He decides to test a new whiz bang software program in Adam's office to see if it helps the bottom line. He notifies Adam that a vendor rep will arrive on Monday morning to train the staff on the new software. Adam passes the information to Adelaide.

Monday morning, the vendor rep shows up to begin the training. Adelaide sails into the conference room almost 30 minutes late and majestically informs the vendor rep to start over.

The vendor rep quickly recaps half of her scheduled 60-minute presentation. As she highlights each feature, she asks attendees to imagine how the feature can improve their efficiency.

The vendor rep soon notices that everyone is watching Adelaide. If she nods, the comments are positive. If she shakes her head, the others say they can't use the software feature. It's obvious that Adelaide would rather eat broken glass than adopt the new software. The vendor rep limps on to the end of her allotted time and wraps up the meeting. The vendor rep has promised to give a status report to Adam's boss.

What kind of report could the vendor rep give to Adam's boss?

1. She could lie and say the training went well, knowing her company has a big contract at stake.
2. She could say that Adelaide is determined to block the use of the new software.
3. She could decide to not give any report since she plans to

ditch the sales career in favor of hanging out at the airport with the Hari Krishnas.

In the actual situation, the senior manager was angry that his pet project was shot down and he fired both the executive assistant and the branch manager. Unfortunately, he failed to follow the company's written HR policies when he fired them; but that's a different story.

Me! Me! Me!

The Pig

Every workplace has one! They appear in all genders.

It's Monday morning and Christine knows that sitting in rush hour traffic will be the high point of her day. After that, she'll suffer a fate almost like death as she sits through the monthly staff meeting. Ms. Piggy will be holding court as usual.

Ms. Piggy is a co-worker who pretends to be a team player. Beneath the friendly smiles lurks a self-centered prima donna. She knows her life is so much more interesting than others. For the past six months she's been monopolizing the staff meetings with the same tale of a product vendor who can't deliver the quality of work she demands.

Initially, Christine and several other managers suggested ways for Ms. Piggy to solve her vendor problem. Ms. Piggy made it clear that their solutions would work fine for idiots like them, but not for her since her work is much more technically sensitive.

Edward, the division head, doesn't know how to handle Ms. Piggy. He wasn't promoted based on his people skills and he doesn't want to get stuck in sticky people problems. He would rather walk across hot coals bare-foot or participate again in the pie eating contest at the company picnic.

Christine arrives at work and grabs a giant mug of coffee on her way to the conference room. Edward slides into the chair at the head of the table and begins asking for updates. Everyone tenses as he reaches Ms. Piggy. Ms. Piggy begins her usual quick update with the usual digressions.

Within a minute the energy level in the room plummets deeper than the Grand Canyon. The guy sitting next to Christine begins playing a game on his phone. Two managers begin reading their emails on their iPads. Edward opens his mouth to cut off Ms. Piggy but she raises her voice and continues. Christine slurps her coffee and tries to keep her head from exploding.

What options are available to Christine?

1. She can fall to the floor pretending to have a seizure so that the meeting ends.
2. She can leap to her feet shrieking "I can't take it anymore. Shut up"!
3. She can suggest that they imitate business networking groups by timing responses so that the staff meetings finish on time and they avoid Ms. Piggy moments.

The above scenario is a composite of too many meetings at too many companies. HR can help managers avoid these ghastly events by training them how to give effective feedback to their subordinates on appropriate office behavior and by urging senior management to pay for coaching for managers who lack people skills.

The Back Stabber

The Coyote

> This story was inspired by a couple of co-workers who had trouble setting appropriate boundaries between their personal and professional lives. They were infuriated when their confidante turned out to be untrustworthy.

Marcella was happy to find a friend like Barry when she joined her new employer. He seemed like such a nice guy, interested in mentoring younger co-workers like her. Barry was a big help to her as she navigated the internal politics of her new employer.

Gradually over the months, Marcella talked about her children and she even gave Barry a few details about her messy divorce. A female co-worker warned Marcella that Barry's nice guy image was barely skin deep. Marcella dismissed the comments as sour grapes because the co-worker had been bounced from Barry's team due to poor performance.

Then Marcella disagrees with Barry about how to solve a problem on their team project. Barry first tries to shame Marcella in front of the other team members by explaining that he has so much more experience than her, his solution is the best. When Marcella refuses to back down, the matter escalates to their boss who agrees with Marcella's solution to the problem.

A week later, the boss stops by Marcella's office to ask if everything is okay at home. He assures her that she can have time off to go to court to deal with her son's drug problem. Marcella is shocked; her son doesn't have a drug problem. Other co-workers stop by during the next few days to offer support.

Marcella remembers confiding to Barry several months ago that she was worried about some of her son's friends. During that conversation she also said she was happy that her son's school invited a community outreach police officer to talk to the students about the consequences of drug use. Marcella thinks that Barry twisted this information because he is mad about losing their disagreement on the team project.

What should Marcella do next?

1. She can confront Barry to ask if he is the source of the rumor and then emulate Dolly Parton in the movie "9 to 5" (threatening to change him from a rooster to a hen).
2. She can complain to an HR representative but she has no proof Barry started the rumor and it's not clear that any employee policy has actually been violated.
3. She can avoid Barry as much as possible and never confide

personal information to him again.

In the actual situation, the backstabbing employee eventually alienated so many employees that he became completely isolated. When the company downsized, he was the only one not invited to join one of the new ventures started by his coworkers.

I Thought We Were Friends

The Scorpion

> This story was inspired by an encounter I had with a co-worker. She was a tall, willowy fashionista. She "teased" men and women about their clothes, their appearance, and any other chink in their armor. Her "teasing" was a cover for her own lack of confidence.

Rebecca is a real pain. She seems nice when people first meet her. But her former boss once compared her to a cancerous cell or a virus, spreading evil in the company. Abby agrees.

Rebecca was the first person to befriend her when Abby began working for the company. Abby was so grateful that it was several months before she realized that every encounter with Rebecca left her deeply depressed, often on the verge of tears. Abby is self-conscious about her weight and a speech impediment that causes her to slur words like Sylvester the cat. Rebecca has a way of drawing attention to all Abby's most sensitive characteristics.

Rebecca once begged Abby to walk with her to the coffee shop because, Rebecca said, she didn't want to go alone. While waiting on her latte, Rebecca picked up a muffin for her breakfast. Suddenly she turned to Abby and said "Here, this is too fattening. You eat it. I'll get myself a banana." Abby was so shocked she couldn't explain that she had already eaten breakfast at home. She felt humiliated because the cashier overheard Rebecca's comment.

Rebecca often imitates Abby's speech impediment, especially if there's an audience. Abby has told Rebecca to stop it because it is not nice to mock people. Rebecca says she's just "picking at" Abby and doesn't mean any harm. Rebecca also accuses Abby of being too sensitive. It all leaves Abby feeling like every misunderstanding is her fault.

After one humiliating episode, Michelle, the HR rep, discovers Abby crying in the bathroom. Michelle is exasperated with Abby's lachrymose acceptance of Rebecca's special brand of friendship. But now that she's seen Abby crying, Michelle knows she needs to take action. She meets with Rebecca to remind her of the company's anti-bullying policy. Now Rebecca runs around telling everyone that Abby can't take a joke.

What should Michelle do next?

1. She could tell Abby to stand up for herself and stop being a victim.
2. She could ignore the situation and hope it fixes itself, most probably when Abby quits.
3. She could confer with Rebecca's supervisor about the next

step in progressive discipline.

In the actual situation, Abby never gained confidence and continued to be bullied. Deciding when behavior crosses the invisible line between teasing and aggression is difficult because it all depends on reasonableness. What would a reasonable person think or feel in a similar situation? There are no easy answers but HR can set workplace expectations by training managers and employees on what is acceptable workplace behavior.

Back Off!

The Giraffe

The comments I received on this story made me realize that I'm not the only short person who has to put up with this not-so-subtle intimidation technique. As with many short people, I look up a long way to make eye contact and tell them (sort of politely) to back off.

Dave is taller than most of his co-workers so that he often seems to loom over them during conversations. He also has a habit of standing really close to people when he talks to them, particularly much shorter women. Aline is one of the shortest employees in the office.

Aline claims he often stands toe to toe with her. She can't prove that he's attempting to intimidate her but she has her suspicions. She's only five feet tall and she's used to men, and some women, using their superior height to try to intimidate her. It's been happening since grade school.

She doesn't like it but she refuses to back away. She throws back her head and looks a long way up to meet them eye-to-eye. She told Lisa, the HR manager, that she'd rather have a permanent crick in her neck than get pushed around just because she's shorter than most people. But she admits that it bothers her when her personal space is invaded.

Aline's office is small, not much bigger than a converted closet. Once she's seated behind her desk, she can get out on only one side. Dave has a bad habit of coming into her office and standing at the corner of the desk so that he blocks her into her seat.

Today when he strolls in and stands at the corner of her desk, Aline's not in the mood to be polite. She points to the chair across the desk from her and orders him to sit down. Dave grins and sits down. They begin discussing the project they are working on. Aline periodically looks at some charts.

Dave wants to look at the charts, too. He stands up and says he'll come around the desk to read over her shoulder. Aline's had enough. She picks up the stack of charts and tosses them across the desk to Dave. "You can read them from there," she replies as she orders him back to his seat.

How should Aline handle Dave in the future?

1. She can kick him in the shins when he stands too close.
2. She can refuse to work with him and probably get stuck with an even more annoying co-worker.
3. She can accept that every job has its petty annoyances and drink more wine each evening.

In the actual situation, Dave reduced his habit of looming over Aline. Looming over shorter co-workers could be considered bullying depending on the circumstances. There are no easy answers to resolving these types of subtly aggressive behavior because there are often no witnesses or the witnesses interpret the incident differently than the recipient of the behavior. HR training on bullying and micro-aggression can explain what is acceptable but training needs to be supported by management to be effective.

Have I Got a Deal for You!

The Weasel

> This story was inspired by one of my co-workers who finally lost patience with a crazy co-worker. She created a fake resume and mass mailed it to every competitor in hopes of ridding our office of the nut. That incident was the kernel of truth from which this story grew.

Cyndi has settled well into her new role as a manager at her company. Her friendly attitude is helping her build solid client relationships. But Tom, the candidate who lost out when Cyndi was promoted, is nursing his sense of injustice.

Tom believes he was the victim of reverse discrimination. He thinks the company promoted Cyndi because they were scared by a former employee's gender discrimination lawsuit. Initially, he sulked and nursed his wounded ego. But he's not stupid; he knows that sulking won't help him. So he does what any reasonably intelligent schemer does. He dreams up a diabolically clever plan to get even.

First, he taps his network within the company to find out where there might soon be an opening for a manager. He learns that Stuart is retiring from his managerial slot as head of internal procurement. It's an important job within the company but a graveyard for career aspirations. No procurement manager has ever received a promotion to the C-suite.

Tom begins maneuvering to have Cyndi promoted to Stuart's soon-to-be-vacated job. Tom persuades a friend to encourage Cyndi to apply for Stuart's job. He also anonymously encourages the HR manager to believe that Cyndi wants Stuart's job. As a result, Cyndi is subjected to nudges, winks, and "discreet" inquiries about her interest in replacing Stuart.

Cyndi is flattered by all the attention. It's nice to be wanted. She knows that if she takes the job, she will be the head of an entire department and get a slight bump in pay.

But Cyndi isn't stupid either. She knows she's got a management job on the production (i.e., revenue producing) side of the business. Procurement is a cost center and not a revenue producer for the company. She knows that production-side managers are more likely to get promoted.

What should Cyndi do next?

1. She can apply for Stuart's job so that she becomes the head of a department and gets the bump in pay; but accept that she'll probably never get another promotion.
2. She can recognize the Machiavellian plot to derail her career and start a counter campaign to get Tom promoted to the

procurement job.

3. She can hang on to her current managerial post and work toward a C-suite promotion.

In the actual situation, Cyndi consulted her most trusted friends who advised her to stick with her current post as the most likely route to the C-suite. Office politics are a feature of every company. For some it's a game that alleviates the boredom of their jobs while others see politicking as war with winners and losers. To limit the damage caused by politicking, HR policies should create objective criteria for performance reviews and promotions which are fairly applied to all employees.

It Rhymes With Witch

The Skunk

This story was inspired by an incident involving a friend of mine. The nasty co-worker wasn't qualified to do my friend's job but that didn't stop her from bullying the boss into trying to ruin my friend's career. My friend got the last laugh. She left a dysfunctional office for a much more satisfying and successful career.

Once upon a time in a town not so far away, there lived a nice woman named Alanis. She liked her job and was always willing to learn from more experienced co-workers. Her boss loved her too and wrote embarrassingly glowing performance reviews.

But there is an evil being in most stories. A wicked witch named Winnie also works in the office. Winnie's not qualified to do the job Alanis was hired for but that doesn't stop her from trying to take over. Winnie smiles in Alanis' face even as she secretly sharpens her talons.

Winnie's opportunity soon arrives. At a staff meeting, their boss, Julia, announces that the company is rolling out a new service and asks Alanis to take the lead for their department. Winnie's death-ray glare bores into Alanis' skull across the conference room table. After the meeting, Winnie loudly announces in the break room that the new project is doomed because Alanis is incompetent.

A week later, Alanis' project notes mysteriously disappear from the system's shared drive. Fortunately, she printed a copy first and is able to recreate her notes. She saves a copy of the new version on a thumb drive. Sure enough, the shared drive version disappears again.

At the next staff meeting, Julia asks Alanis why she doesn't share information with the rest of the group. Alanis reports the mysterious deletions and asks that IT investigate the deletions. Co-workers look at Winnie then quickly look away. Julia abruptly ends the meeting.

The next day, Julia calls Alanis to her office. Winnie is waiting in Julia's office. Julia says that she's decided to appoint Winnie as co-chair of the project because it's obviously too much for Alanis to do alone. Winnie smirks as she demands copies of all Alanis' notes.

After that, Winnie changes the entire strategy so that their department misses deadlines set by Julia's bosses. Winnie blames Alanis and complains about a lack of cooperation. Alanis is again called to Julia's office where she is criticized for disloyalty and undermining the department. Julia says Alanis can resign or be fired.

What should Alanis do next?

1. She can continue to protest her innocence knowing she won't win since a weak manager is as dangerous as a witch.
2. She can booby trap Winnie's desk with eau de skunk.
3. She can resign and consult a lawyer about whether she has

grounds for suing the company but lawyers cost more than what she earned while still employed.

In the actual situation, the targeted employee resigned. Any office can develop an infestation of wicked witches if management is weak. Unfortunately, no HR policy can prevent problems caused by a poor corporate culture that rewards Winnie and punishes Alanis.

New Job; Old Baggage

The Whitetail Deer

> This story was inspired by two incidents. One incident arose when a family member volunteered at a local non-profit only to receive the Heathers treatment from a couple of other volunteers. The other incident was based on my experience as the new hire in an office run by a clique.
> We can't escape ourselves. In hindsight, I realize it took me a while to understand that. I now mentor a couple of younger women about not letting their kneejerk reactions based on past experiences screw up their careers.

Betty started a new job about six months ago but already the old patterns are starting to repeat. Betty's last job became so unbearable that she quit. Now she seems to be headed down the same path again.

At her last job, a clique of female co-workers proved that "Heathers" don't get nicer as they grow up; they just get older. ("Heathers" is a 1988 cult film about some very bad high school girls.) They made Betty miserable. They invited her to lunch during her first week on the job for the apparent purpose of mocking her interests and lifestyle. That was the beginning of a long campaign of passive aggressive behavior aimed at undermining Betty.

When Betty complained about misplaced files or sabotaged resources, her clueless boss labeled her a complainer. Betty didn't want to be best friends with the clique, but in a small office she was isolated and alone. Betty's confidence eroded and her performance suffered. When her performance review assessed her as "not a team player," Betty took the hint and found her current job.

Unfortunately, the old baggage came with her. She knows some of her new co-workers think she's a snob for declining lunch invitations and not participating in the monthly office birthday parties. But Betty is cautious of getting to know her new co-workers because she's afraid of meeting a new group of Heathers.

Today, an HR rep asked Betty to stop by. At their meeting, the HR rep asked Betty how she liked her office, her workload, and how she was getting along with her colleagues. Betty gave a non-committal answer. Then the HR rep asked Betty if she would like to participate in a new mentoring program that was created to help new employees integrate into the company.

What should Betty do next?

1. She can decide based on her past experiences that she will "fail" at this job so she should quit now and join a commune in Alaska.
2. She can start looking for another job hoping that things will be different next time.

3. She can accept the invitation to join the mentoring program, increasing her chances of having a satisfying career with her current employer.

In the actual case, the first employer had no mentoring program because the owners were not convinced that touchy-feely programs contributed to the bottom line. Consequently, they experienced a high level of employee churn and were eventually acquired by a competitor. The second employer successfully piloted a mentoring program in hopes of improving employee loyalty and retention.

Make Her Go Away!

The Donkey

> This story was inspired by several accomplished women for whom no achievement is ever enough. Their insecurities cause them to feel threatened and jealous of everyone they meet, particularly other women. As a friend told me long ago, "some women are their own worst enemies".

Jane drags herself into work the first day after the holidays, not sure whether she wants to be here. She's the HR manager for her company and she knows that her co-workers will return with a host of problems. She has a few of her own.

Her house is still trashed from hosting her family's holiday dinner. Her widowed mom chose the holiday dinner to announce that she planned to take an around-the-world trip with Frederik, a gigolo she met on her most recent Caribbean cruise. Jane's daughter wants to ditch her senior year in high school to join a religious commune. On Christmas Day, the Christmas lights shorted out causing a fire that scorched half the front porch.

Upon reflection, Jane decides she is happy to be at work as she pours her first cup of coffee. She slides into her ergonomically designed chair and sighs as she begins reviewing her email inbox which filled up while she was on vacation. Sure enough, there's an email from Doris.

Doris is complaining that another manager interfered with Doris' subordinates. The other manager, Lara, is a relatively new hire and Doris is "concerned" that Lara doesn't understand that Doris makes all the decisions in her department. Doris demands that Jane tell Lara to stay away from Doris' department or face immediate dismissal.

Jane sighs heavily. People who don't know Doris well think she's charming. She has perfect clothes, hair, makeup, and a smile. But Jane knows that image is no more than Hollywood special effects. Underneath, Doris is as vicious as a junkyard dog when it comes to defending her turf. She bullies anyone she sees as a threat to her career.

Jane knows that Doris' bullying arises from insecurity, which seems nonsensical with her talent and ability. Jane stares at Doris' email and wonders how to respond.

What are Jane's options?

1. She can file Doris' email with all the previous complaints in a cyberspace trash bin.
2. She can relieve her frustrations at Doris' bullying by implying that senior management believes Doris is the past and Lara is the future.

3. She can have a quiet word with Doris, stressing that the company recognizes her value but that constant complaints won't help her career aspirations.

In the actual situation, the insecure employee continued to bully her co-workers whenever she felt threatened. But she became increasingly isolated and even senior management began to notice that no one wanted to work with her as her bullying reputation spread through the workforce.

III

Office Romances

Looking For Love

The Baboon

> This story was inspired by two co-workers. Workplace romances historically meant that the lower level person, usually the female, watched her career nosedive along with her personal reputation. The #MeToo movement is beginning to change cultural expectations of what is acceptable behavior in the workplace.

Once upon a time a woman named Trish was searching for true love. Like so many others, she found it at the office. Her Prince Charming was John, VP in another division of the company. John was also looking for true love having just wrapped up a nasty divorce with his former true love.

Trish met John at the office Christmas Party and thought he was a jerk. She changed her mind at the summer picnic when she saw him playing with his kids and lobbing water balloons at other managers. John looked like an Olympic athlete compared to some of the other managers.

So when John's division needed a little extra help with a special project, Trish volunteered. By diligent effort, Trish made herself a star on John's team and managed to catch his eye. A shared interest in the project led to a little flirting which led to long dinners and then to other extracurricular activities.

Alas, as with every fairytale a curse fell upon the lovers. John's schedule kept him busy with out-of-town business trips and Trish began to feel neglected. John tired of her whining over the dinner wine about how his career meant more to him than she did, giving John nasty flashbacks to his ex-wife's complaints.

As in a fairytale, when a workplace romance fizzles people behave badly. John stopped responding to her emails and text messages. He also told Trish's boss that Trish could never work in his division again because she was a lousy worker. Meanwhile, Trish's performance nosedived as she realized her fairytale was fizzling.

The final fizzle arrives when Trish hears through the grapevine that John is blacklisting her. She's convinced it is retaliation for their affair. When her boss counsels her about her cratering performance, Trish remembers that he is John's friend. Trish storms into HR Manager Billie Jean's office to complain about sexual harassment and retaliation.

What options are available to Billie Jean?

1. She can slap the taste buds out of John's mouth for being stupid since managers are expected to use their brains to make decisions at the office.

2. She can recommend settling Trish's claims to limit the damage caused by John's violations of company policy.
3. She can disguise the details and include them in her next popular bodice-ripper novel, which she hopes will earn her enough money to retire early.

In the actual situation, the manager was counseled for violating HR policies. He had wrecked his chances at a promotion. The woman accepted a settlement of her claims and left the company still looking for true love. Every company should have a "no fraternization" HR policy, preferably before love turns to hate, that explains how the company will handle these messy situations.

Will He Or Won't He?

The Tiger

> This story was inspired by the failed romance of a frenemy. Her steady Eddy took her to their favorite restaurant to make his big announcement knowing she wouldn't cause a public scene.

For weeks, Karen has been skipping merrily around the office. Her subordinates agree they've never seen her so approachable, so agreeable, so nice. When Sherry knocked her coffee mug, spilling herbal tea all over a report, Karen only smiled benignly. On an average day, Karen would have screeched like a banshee about clumsiness and smashed the coffee mug.

What has mellowed out their normally high-strung boss, they wonder. Little do they know that Karen is expecting a big announcement from her boyfriend, Dean. They've been dating for years and lately Karen has noticed some changes in Dean's behavior. She thinks it means that he's finally going to pop the question.

It's Valentine's Day and Karen has nudged Dean into remembering to invite her to dinner at her favorite restaurant. All day Karen mentally rehearses who she wants to invite to the wedding and who she wants as bridesmaids. Karen meets Dean at the restaurant because he says he won't have time to swing by and pick her up. At the restaurant, Dean sits deep in thought for much of the meal. Karen waits impatiently for the big moment. She drops a couple of broad hints about an autumn wedding.

Finally, as dessert and coffee arrives, Dean begins talking. He tells Karen that he's met someone else. Actually, it's a long-time co-worker of his that he's finally noticed after years of working side by side. He tells Karen that this is their last evening together. He hands over his key to the condo as he tells her that he's already collected his personal stuff from her condo while she was at work.

Karen listens in disbelief. Suddenly it all becomes clear to her. She had to drive alone to the restaurant. He agreed to her favorite restaurant because he knew she wouldn't make a public scene in her favorite restaurant.

What will happen to Karen's subordinates now that their boss has been crushed by the light of the moon? Find out in the next installment of "He Loves Me, He Loves Me Not".

The Morning After

The Tiger Cub

> As previously noted, this two-part story was inspired by a frenemy. Fortunately, my frenemy wasn't a supervisor when she was dumped by her boyfriend, since the HR rep was based about 1000 miles away at the main office.

Karen expected her long-time boyfriend to pop the question at a special Valentine's Day dinner. Instead, he dumped her with the dessert. Karen drove home in shock and drank a whole bottle of red wine while she tried to figure out where it all went wrong. She dug out her secret stash of dark chocolates but some things can't be fixed even by chocolate.

Karen awoke to a hangover and a feeling of being watched. She rolled over to find her cat observing her with lofty disdain. She briefly contemplated calling in sick but bosses should lead by example, or so she's been told. So she dragged herself out of bed, swallowed several aspirin, and trudged out the door to work.

At the office, Karen literally ran into Sherry when they rounded the same corner from opposite directions. Sherry's hot herbal tea splashed generously over both of them. Karen snarled and pushed past Sherry, who tottered back to her cubicle to have hysterics.

Jim glanced at Sherry across the cubicle wall thinking that he ought to do something. But he wasn't any good at helping his wife when she cried so what could he do for a co-worker? He dropped to the floor and crawled on hands and knees toward the exit. Sue vaulted a low cubicle wall to evade Karen and ran down the hall to the HR rep's office.

Meanwhile, Teresa, the HR rep, is sitting quietly at her desk, feeling good about life, when Sue caroms off the door jamb, bounces against the bookcase, and drops into a chair gasping for air. Teresa studies her in gathering alarm. Sue's shin is bleeding and one shoe is missing.

Sue says Karen has finally had the big mental break with reality that her subordinates have been betting on for months. Teresa listens helplessly. Her HR training didn't really prepare her for these sorts of emergencies.

What should Teresa, the HR rep, do next?

1. She can hide in her office and hope the situation resolves itself.
2. She can join Karen's subordinates in texting alerts to each other warning when Karen leaves her office to search for victims to criticize.
3. She can go down the hall to investigate and to assess whether

Karen needs some personal leave to recover her composure.

In the actual situation, employees hid from the jilted lover in less dramatic fashion. When the personal dramas of employees spill over to the workplace, HR can help by taking swift action to intervene and mitigate workplace disruptions. For example, the HR rep could encourage the jilted employee to contact the employee assistance program (EAP) for a referral to a mental health counselor.

See, What Happened Was...

The Otters

> This story is an adaptation of a lively tale told by a friend of mine who was a chaperon at the summer party hosted by his then-employer, a prominent Louisiana law firm. All these years later, I still giggle when I remember his recounting of the harrowing details and the aftermath (total prohibition on intern parties).

Lexington & Concord is a professional firm that hires summer interns every year. El Cee, as it's fondly known, has a reputation for training summer interns by making them work long hours with minimal feedback on their performance. Interns are happy to suffer knowing that if they survive, they will increase their chances of receiving a good job offer.

Kate, the HR manager, thinks the summer interns should be rewarded for their hard work. She convinces Charles, the senior partner, to have an end-of-summer party for the interns. Charles reluctantly agrees.

The party is held at the home of Rob, a senior partner in the firm who likes to brag about his possessions. Unfortunately, Rob and his wife, Sally, choose this day to enact their version of the War of the Roses.

The guests arrive in time to watch Sally yanking off her wedding ring and hurling it into the shrubbery. The members of the firm are used to the Rob and Sally soap opera and swerve around the fight with the ease of practice, headed for the drinks by the pool.

Kate quickly steers the interns to the outdoor kitchen and pool area. After asking several partners to chaperon the interns she dashes away to break up the hosts' fight before the neighbors call the cops. She finds Sally sobbing hysterically but Rob has vanished.

When Kate returns to the pool, she spies Rob propped against the shoulder of a young intern. As she approaches, Kate hears him making suggestions to the young lady that freeze the marrow in her HR bones. Before the intern can respond, Kate grabs Rob's elbow to drag him away. Unfortunately, he staggers against Kate. They both topple into the pool.

Several people dive in to rescue them. Kate clambers out of the pool and looks around in horror. Her summer party is turning into a Roman orgy with half-naked people frolicking at poolside.

Now it's Monday morning and Kate is in Charles' office trying to explain what happened at the party. What should she say?

1. She can say she's resigning to start a new career as an event planner.
2. She can imply that it's Charles' fault for not attending and

using the force of his disapproval to keep everyone in line.

3. She can promise to never again share her ideas for boosting morale.

In the actual situation, the firm banned parties for summer interns. HR professionals can help their companies by setting clear guidelines on behavior at company-sponsored events.

IV

Millennials

Can We Get By Without Her?

The Lizard

> This story is based on a true story from a friend who interrupted her presentation to tell the employee that name-calling was inappropriate and wouldn't change the fact that the company had changed procedures. My friend was much nicer than I would have been to the disrespectful subordinate.
> This story is depressingly common in industries that rely on low wage, unskilled labor. Such industries are dominated by companies that operate on shoestring budgets and have no resources to solve their staffing issues.

Georgia is the manager of a group home for disabled adults. It's not easy caring for people who have trouble remembering what they did five minutes ago or who need help with what is euphemistically called "life activities". But they are a breeze compared to dealing with employees.

Job seekers who can stomach the idea of helping with bathing, cooking, and light housekeeping usually disappear when they hear about the pay. It's not that families of the disabled don't care about their loved ones but they usually have no idea of the true cost of care. Or as Georgia's boss constantly complains, everyone wants Cadillac coverage for the price of a Chevy.

The latest employee through the revolving door is Krystal, a twenty-something whose parents stopped paying her cell phone bill and put a padlock on the refrigerator. Taking the hint, Krystal realized that her parents wanted her to get a job.

Krystal is a so-so employee. Georgia puts up with her because the home is usually short-staffed. But Georgia resents spending so much of her time trying to motivate Krystal to do the bare minimum in her job description.

Last week, Georgia learned that Krystal had again failed to take Lenny, one of the disabled adults, to his favorite restaurant. First, Krystal said she forgot. But when Georgia stared silently at her, she broke down and admitted that she didn't feel like eating greasy food with Lenny. Georgia's blood pressure spiked. She retorted that Krystal didn't have to eat the food; she just needed to drive Lenny to the restaurant so that he could.

Today, the employees are gathered for the monthly staff meeting. Georgia reviews a recent situation where one of their charges was injured when he tripped over the TV remote that was lying on the floor. She explains new procedures that the company wants them to follow to avoid a repeat injury.

Georgia asks the employees if they understand the new procedures. Krystal rolls her eyes and mutters audibly "bitch". Everyone turns to look at her. Then they look at Georgia.

What should Georgia do next?

1. She can lean across the table and slap the taste out of Krystal's mouth.
2. She can fire Krystal and escort her off the premises with a well-placed kick in the rear.
3. She can remember how short-staffed they are and give Krystal a written reprimand and a second chance.

In the actual situation, the company gave the insubordinate employee a second chance based on staff shortages. But they started the search for a replacement.

Hey, Y'all, I'd Like a Job

The Puppy

> This story was inspired by a friend of mine, also a small business owner, who showed me a copy of the email. She said, "Here's your next blog!" I've changed some of the details to protect the poor little waif who wrote it.

It's been a long day and Mary is catching up on her emails. As she deletes all the unsolicited introductions from sales people trying to sell her stuff she either doesn't want or can't afford, she wonders again if she was completely nuts to open her own business.

When she's not avoiding obnoxious sales pitches, she's dealing with job seekers. She can track the college graduation season simply by the number of unsolicited emails she receives. She rarely reads the attached resumes because of the first impressions created by the emails. The smart graduates use proper grammar and complete sentences in their emails. The smartest graduates actually look at her company website to see what kind of business she runs.

She sighs and clicks on the next email. Its contents strike her so forcibly that she takes a big swig of her single malt scotch. She glances out the window to see if it's a full moon; it's not. It's also too early for the solar eclipse. No natural phenomenon explains the email she's reading.

The email says, "Hey, y'all, I just graduated from college and I'd love to come work for you if you've got an opening. If you don't have any jobs right now, please keep me in mind when you do. Thx, Candace".

Mary has received some strange introductions from job-seekers. She was once chased two city blocks until she realized the crazy man running after her wasn't a stalker; he was trying to hand deliver his resume. She's had friends ask her to hire their college-aged children because some of those young people are otherwise unemployable.

Mary knows that millennials are much more informal than her generation of workers. But Candace's email introduction surely takes the prize. This clueless waif graduated from college without ever learning how to present herself to a potential employer.

What should Mary do next?

1. She can hit delete and ignore Candace because it's not her responsibility to teach millennials how to apply for a job.
2. She can drink more scotch and save the email for the bad days when she needs a quick laugh.
3. She can remember her own job-hunting mistakes and email Candace some kind advice on how the power of first impressions affects gainful employment.

In the actual situation, the business owner never responded to the college student and the college graduate never followed up on the initial email. Informality is preferable to the strict workplace hierarchies of the past that stifled innovation and creativity. However, informality should never cross the line into disrespect. HR departments can help by collaborating with college placement offices to teach soon-to-be-graduates how to properly approach prospective employers.

Welcome To The Real World

The Squirrel

> This story was inspired by the experiences of a couple of millennials who failed to understand that pitching ideas to the boss is different than engaging in a dialogue with their college professors.

Brooke is a millennial who was recently assigned to Sandy's department. Sandy likes working with younger people who are natives of the digital world and can show her how to use her smart phone apps. They are young and enthusiastic, and some, like Brooke, are idealists.

Brooke wants to change the world. After college, her parents supported her for an additional year so she could work at a non-profit. Her record of clever ideas for the non-profit helped her get hired at Sandy's company.

In her first week, Brooke suggests some relatively inexpensive software upgrades that improve efficiency and save money. Most of the savings come from job cuts as tasks are automated. The older workers who are let go aren't qualified for other open positions and management cut the training budget back around the time Brooke was born. Brooke doesn't notice the job losses because she's on to her next big idea.

Her next big idea is an IT systems upgrade that could save the entire company millions of dollars. Unfortunately, the upgrade will also cost tens of millions of dollars, require the company to shut down entirely for six months, and cause massive job cuts. She announces her idea to Sandy's boss, Bob. He thanks Brooke and boots her out of his office.

Brooke doesn't understand how Bob can be so dim-witted as not to see the long-term benefits. She won't listen to Bob or Sandy when they tell her that the company simply can't afford to give up six months of sales to rebuild IT systems from scratch.

Brooke thinks that Bob and Sandy are being negative because they are dinosaurs who don't "get" new technology and how it improves the world. Brooke decides she needs to bypass the unenlightened ones and go straight to the top. She tells Sandy that she wants to pitch her idea to the company president.

What advice should Sandy give to Brooke?

1. She can encourage Brooke and then watch as the company president explodes like a geyser at the thought of losing six months' revenue.
2. She can suggest that Brooke drink fewer cappuccinos and increase her wine consumption in the hopes she will have

fewer brilliant ideas.

3. She can tell Brooke that the company president will be more receptive to her ideas if she can come up with a plan to offset the short term costs.

In the actual situation, the millennial did not listen to Sandy's advice and presented her idea to the company president with results that were foreseeable to everyone except Brooke. Idealism is a wonderful quality but not necessarily in the workplace. HR should use the on-boarding process to help millennials transition from college to the workplace.

I Want My Dream Job!

The Blind Mole

This story was inspired by a millennial subordinate who didn't know how to find the supply closet to get more staples. He was also found one day staring blankly at the copier which had run out of paper. He had a 4-year university degree and a graduate degree.

Ashleigh is one of the newest employees of the company and she's making waves. Some co-workers think she's arrogant and rude; others think she's got some great ideas but lacks communication skills. Everyone has an opinion of Ashleigh.

Polly, the HR rep, hears all these conflicting opinions and wonders if she ought to step in to do some quick counseling with Ashleigh. Polly is the mother of several millennials and thinks she knows how to talk to them. While she's trying to decide, Ashleigh's manager stomps into her office breathing hard through clenched teeth.

Tom says he's had it with Ashleigh. He asks Polly if there is an exception in the HR policies that would allow him to punt Ashleigh into outer space. What has happened, she asks. His knuckles whiten as he grips the arm rests of his chair citing examples of Ashleigh's unacceptable behavior.

Ashleigh refuses to stop fiddling with her smart phone or tablet during staff meetings. She is apparently incapable of typing in any format except text messaging. She has a short attention span and often interrupts discussions to ask about irrelevant details. But what really pushes Tom's buttons is Ashleigh's inability to solve problems.

Last week, she showed Tom her stapler and said it was out of staples. When he told her to go to the supply closet to get a refill, she stared blankly as if she'd never heard of the concept of resupply.

Yesterday he found Ashleigh standing at the copier staring at the flashing lights with a puzzled frown. She said the copier wasn't working. The copier was out of paper and Ashleigh didn't know how to add more paper. That's when Tom decided she needs to go.

Polly invites Ashleigh to a follow up meeting as part of the on-boarding process. Ashleigh admits she's having trouble because the job is "hard" and Tom is "mean" to her. Ashleigh says she wishes she had followed her college professor's advice and held out for her dream job.

What should Polly do next?

1. She can explain to Ashleigh that finding her "dream job" at 21 is a fantasy because she lacks the life experience to recognize her dream job.
2. She can write off Ashleigh as a pampered princess and begin

searching for a replacement.

3. She can encourage Ashleigh to persevere and learn practical skills, such as how to reload the copier's paper tray.

In the actual situation, Ashleigh voluntarily left to continue her quest for her dream job. Every employer with millennials has noticed that their attitude to work is different from baby boomers. HR can smooth the learning curve with a robust on-boarding process that explains what behavior is acceptable in the workplace and with a mentoring program.

The Not-So-Little Prince

The Gazelle

> This story was inspired by a friend's tale of her workplace where the 70+ year-old owner struggles to understand his employees who have more in common with his grandchildren than him. My friend is the mother of millennials and interprets between generations.

Vicky is the HR person for her company because her business partners are guys who would rather face a starving lion bare-handed than deal with employees. Lately she's been seesawing between the urge to kill one of the younger workers or just knock his block off.

Gus is a 30-something millennial who thinks he is a prince who can set his own rules. So Gus ignores the rule that he should show up on time every work day. He ignores the rule that he should tell his supervisor if he leaves the office during the workday.

Vicky learns that Gus has continued to ignore her verbal warnings when she receives a phone call from Frank, the company founder.

Frank is a brilliant man but he refuses to learn how to use an electronic calendar, his email account, or the Internet. When Frank started his career, people actually talked to each other. He sees no reason to change his work habits now.

Frank asks if she declared a work holiday without telling him because he's alone in the office and needs help with the copier. Vicky is flummoxed. She runs through the list of all twenty employees while Frank breathes heavily down the phone line. Two employees always take a late lunch. Several more are off-site at client meetings. But the other employees should be in the office, including Gus.

The next day, Vicky calls Gus to her office. Gus arrives twenty minutes late and slouches into a chair. He takes a deep gulp of his energy drink, bored and disinterested, and demands an explanation for being dragged away from his work.

Vicky stares at him through a red haze. The last time a young male addressed her in such a surly tone, he got whapped up-side the head and lost his driving privileges for a month. But her son was sixteen at the time. With superhuman strength Vicky restrains herself.

She explains to the oblivious Gus that their small staff requires collaboration and that means notifying others when he leaves the office. Gus drains his energy drink and tosses the container in the trash, splashing Vicky's foot. He suggests that Frank should be given an iPad with everyone's calendar loaded on it. Then he would know where all his staff is at any time. Vicky feels the red haze gathering again.

What options are available to Vicky?

1. She can congratulate herself on her self-restraint for letting Gus live.
2. She can look around for a frenemy who can be conned into hiring Gus.
3. She can give Gus a final warning but begin planning to replace him.

In the actual situation, the millennial was given another chance to improve. He is apparently still unaware of how close he is to termination for cause. HR can help integrate younger workers through orientation meetings that explain what employers expect from permanent, full-time employees. Some college graduates mistakenly believe that permanent employment is no different than college internships.

Improving Morale With Beatings

The Long Horn Cattle

> This story was inspired by a prospective client, a social media company. It turned out that the senior management team was as conflicted as the rest of the team about how to be socially responsible. They are still in business and still chaotic with frequent staff turnover.

Earl started his tech company in the depths of the financial meltdown a few years ago. After years of struggling, he expanded his client base to the point that he now has employees instead of subbing out the work to independent contractors.

Earl ought to feel happy, but he's not. His employees make him unhappy. He hired millennials expecting them to be energetic and creative and to keep his company on the cutting edge of technology. Instead, they infuriate him with their attitude.

Greg and Sam blew a deadline because they went bar-hopping with college friends. They had not wanted to work on the project but they were next up on the rotation for assignments. So Earl ignored their lack of enthusiasm and told them to get busy. Their final work product was so crappy that Earl agreed not to charge the client.

Earl was so angry he decided to take away a few perks. He folded up the ping pong table and shoved it in the storeroom. Then he ordered Greg and Sam to report to the office every day so that he could keep a closer eye on them. Now they sulk at their desks, doing as little as possible, while surfing the web for other job opportunities.

Earl is also annoyed with Beth. Beth wants to work on a fundraising campaign for her favorite non-profit (humane housing for pot-bellied pigs that have outgrown their cuteness) rather than working on client projects. Earl likes bacon and ham and doesn't see any point in coddling a former pet piggy. Besides, he hired Beth to work for his clients, not her favorite charity. He said no.

Morale is so low that even the free-beer-on-Friday promise hasn't improved the general malaise afflicting the office. It's Friday evening. Earl is sitting at home drinking the single malt scotch he reserves for special occasions and wondering what he should do on Monday morning.

What options are available to Earl?
1. He can take away all the perks, including free beer, and enforce more discipline until employees crank out quality work and morale improves.
2. He can fire his current employees and start over with a new batch of employees who accept his way of doing things.

3. He can allow his employees more freedom to choose their assignments and set their own schedules as long as they meet project deadlines and submit quality work.

Small business owners would be wise to catch up with the changing expectations of their workforces, particularly millennials. For example, millennials want to participate in socially beneficial activities. As a result, many companies are developing HR policies on non-profit volunteering. These HR policies vary widely from simply encouraging volunteer work to providing paid leave for volunteer work. Companies hope these policies will improve their ability to attract and retain millennials. An added bonus is that these HR policies are popular with employees of all ages.

V
Holiday Hangovers

Spring Fever

The Robin

> This story was inspired by memories of living in Pennsylvania and upstate New York near Buffalo. The further north one goes, the worse the spring fever. When the forsythia blooms and robins appear, we all expect spring to show up too.

It's been a long, hard winter at Melanie's company with employees stuck in snow drifts or struck down by the flu. Melanie began wondering if her company could survive as deadlines were missed due to understaffing.

Then the sun came out, forsythia and daffodils began blooming, trees showed an aureole of red as they began budding. People shed their heavy winter coats. Alas! A cold snap killed the daffodils and left everyone twitchy as spring seemed never to arrive.

Dan's an optimist and he's been trying to think and practice his golf swing simultaneously, getting ready for spring. Two days ago, as he thought about his brilliant ideas, he swung higher and faster. Suddenly, a horrible thud echoed through the office, followed by a crash and a scream.

Melanie dashed out of her office to find Randy sprawled on the floor clutching his bleeding face. Dan knelt beside him, trying to stop the bleeding while stuffing his golf club under his desk. Melanie hauled Randy to his feet and marched him out the door to her car to drive him to the emergency room. Hours later, she returned to report that Randy needed stitches but would be okay. She banished Dan's golf clubs from the office unless they were locked, out of sight, in his personal vehicle.

Today Randy returned to work and accused Dan of trying to kill him. While Melanie tried to mediate their fight, she heard Karla yelling at Teresa about stinky take-out food. Teresa retorted that her garlicky take-out was less offensive than Karla's cheap perfume fumigating the place, not to mention Karla's dark roots showing because she was too cheap to pay for a salon dye job.

Melanie sailed in to separate Karla and Teresa, closely followed by Dan and Randy hoping to see the office equivalent of a mud wrestling match. Eventually everyone grumpily returned to their desks to sulk.

What can Melanie do to alleviate her employees' spring fever?

1. She can sit in her office, occasionally venting a primal scream of frustration, and hope that scares her employees into doing their jobs.
2. She can buy cheap rum and fruit juice for her staff and tell

them to pretend they're on a beach in an island paradise.

3. She can plan an impromptu outing to take her employees' minds off their troubles as they wait for spring to actually arrive.

Everyone gets cabin fever waiting for spring to actually arrive after months of dreariness and cold weather. HR and management can help with morale boosters to lift everyone's spirits. Morale boosters can be as simple as encouraging everyone to wear bright colors to combat the blues or having an employee appreciation party.

April Fools. Not.

The Wolf

> This story was inspired by my older brother. Many years ago, he was stationed at an Army base where a few of his buddies decided to relieve their boredom with a contest to see who could build the best impromptu weapon. The soda can bazooka won. Don't try this at home! It's much too dangerous.

April Fools' Day was three days ago but some idiots are still pulling pranks. Danny showed up early on Monday with nylon fishing line which he used as a tether for a stuffed mouse he bought at a pet store. The morning was punctuated with screams as he yanked his mouse across the hallway each time the elevator doors opened.

Pam confiscated Danny's mouse and threatened to let his co-workers beat him to a pulp if he tried the same trick on Tuesday. On Tuesday, Danny showed up with whoopee cushions and plastic snakes. By lunch, Pam had collected his entire stash.

This morning, Pam is waiting for Danny in the elevator lobby.

While Danny distracts her, his co-conspirators sneak into the break room to raid the recycling bin in the kitchen. Jim and Barbara are military veterans and they want to create a homemade bazooka they heard about while in the service.

First, they cut the ends off aluminum soda cans and duct tape them into a long tube. Then they poke a hole in the bottom of the last can to create a breach. A crowd of curious co-workers gathers to watch. Barbara stuffs a tennis ball down the tube. Jim produces a cigarette lighter and ignites a spark. With a whoosh and a shoomp, the tennis ball hurtles across the room and smashes a hole in the plasterboard wall. Everyone scatters as Pam runs into the break room.

Pam knows what's really wrong with Danny, Jim, and Barbara. They're bored and restless. The company has been fighting a hostile takeover for months and employees are afraid of job cuts if the takeover happens.

During the slower winter months, everyone simply waited, too cold to care. Now spring is here and employees are twitchy as the takeover saga continues. Management has been very slow about updating employees on what's happening.

What options are available for Pam?

1. She can announce a contest to keep the April Fools' Day practical jokes going for the entire month.
2. She can begin playing her own practical jokes on co-workers to show that HR isn't always the "Department of No".
3. She can suggest that management hold a "town hall" meeting to update employees on the hostile takeover and what it

means for the employees.

In the actual situation, the tennis ball struck a spectator in the forehead knocking him out. Having a little fun to break the monotony and pressure is important. But sometimes hijinks are a symptom of a deeper problem, such as uncertainty due to workplace changes. HR can help by encouraging management to be transparent in their communications with employees. For example, in this story a transparent communications policy could include a weekly update about the anticipated changes in the workplace which would reduce anxiety.

What Did You Do This Weekend?

The Sloth

> This story originally appeared two days after Memorial Day. It was inspired by horror stories recounted by co-workers after a holiday break. To judge by the reaction, every reader could relate to it.

Summer has arrived! Renee, HR manager for her company, walks around the building slurping coffee, taking a head count of the survivors of the Memorial Day weekend. It's ten o'clock in the morning and workers are still straggling in.

Renee sympathizes with her co-workers. She threw her alarm clock across the bedroom this morning. For a moment, she contemplated rolling over and drifting back to sleep. But she had to go back to work sometime, so it might as well be today. As she stepped into the shower, she wondered again why she chose her profession.

Now, as she strolls around the office, she remembers why she likes her job, at least most of the time. People are so interesting. Employees are people and they are acting very interesting this morning.

In the break room, size-4 Tina is bemoaning overeating during a family picnic. She'll get fat, she complains to Fred and Sam. They eye her trim figure and say nothing; they're not stupid. The larger-than-size-4 women glare at her as they pour their coffee. Abby brushes past Tina, accidentally dumping coffee on Tina's sandaled feet. Abby apologizes profusely and refills her mug. The other women smile sourly as Tina swabs her feet with a paper towel.

Renee disappears down the hall before Tina can corner her to complain about Abby. She sees Ben shuffling toward her. He's bright red. He explains that he fell asleep at poolside and his friends thought it was funny to watch him turning pink, then red. He may need to take some time off to recuperate from the sunburn. Renee murmurs sympathetically and turns to greet Ted.

Ted's eyes are red-rimmed and sunken. His coffee mug is the size of a Big Gulp drink. He and his wife have three preschoolers, including a six-month-old baby. Ted mumbles that his 4-year old did a swan dive off the back of the sofa, knocking her teeth loose. The 2-year old exists only to have temper tantrums and the baby has colic. Ted hasn't slept for two days and he's glad as heck to be back to work.

Renee pats his shoulder consolingly and encourages Ted to look forward to the surly teenage years. She watches Ben and Ted shuffle away. Renee sighs and heads for her office.

It's going to be a long, hot summer.

The Morning After

The Grizzly Bear

> This story was inspired by a friend who was a supervisor. Back when I began my professional career, this was a fairly common result of the holidays. But our social and business expectations have evolved and there is much less tolerance for extra-curricular activities that interfere with work performance.

George rolls over and groans. It's the morning after July 4th and he needs to go to work. George would love to call in sick but he's used all his accrued PTO. As he shakily goes through his morning routine, he reflects on the long weekend that was.

George used his last PTO hours to take off Monday, knowing that he planned to have a good time over the weekend with his buddies. His memories of Friday night are fuzzy, involving a sports bar, overpriced drinks, and a contortionist from a circus or a zoo or something. On Saturday his wife dragged him to a picnic with their church group. After gobbling down a couple of hot dogs and a bowl of potato salad, he joined his buddies for another evening of overpriced drinks.

Sunday he recuperated, sort of, staying in bed most of the day. His wife was unhappy because he hadn't managed to do any of the chores that he said he would. She walked around the house humming Highway 101's hit "*Whiskey, If You Were a Woman*". George might be hungover, but he's not stupid. It's almost a relief to go to work today.

George staggers out the door and slides into his car. He makes it to the office safely, parks the car, and gathers his dignity for the stroll into the building. His co-workers smile at him and surreptitiously start a betting pool to guess when he'll collapse face down on his cubicle's desk.

Sally, his manager, notices his shaky hands clutching a mug of coffee in a death grip and frowns. She's been worried for a long time about George. He's a likeable guy, hardworking and knowledgeable when he's sober but it's obvious that he has a problem. Sally consults Connie, the HR manager, and they decide to call George in for a meeting.

What should they say to George?

1. They could berate him for showing up too hung over to do his job and threaten to fire him.
2. They could sanctimoniously point out the obvious, that he's an alcoholic, and needs to change if he wants to keep his job.
3. They could show concern by offering to help him get into a treatment plan to deal with his alcoholism before it costs him his job.

In the actual situation, George was a senior manager whose wife left him due to his inability to stay sober. Holidays can be difficult for employees with addictions. Employers can help their employees, and the company's bottom line, by offering an employee assistance program (EAP) and having an HR policy that encourages treatment first as an alternative to disciplinary proceedings.

What Are You Wearing?

The Toucan

> This story was inspired by one of my former outside consultants who was a fabulous CPA and an escapee from a big accounting firm. He often showed up to our internal meetings wearing shorts and Hawaiian shirts. I learned so much about basic accounting principles and financial best practices from him. I also learned how to use self-employment as a justification for ditching the business suit.
> L.B., this one's for you.

Bob enjoyed his July 4th holiday so much that he hated to come back to work. Today he showed up still dressed for vacation. Cindy, the HR manager, was aghast and choked on a mouthful of coffee when she caught a glimpse of Bob passing in the hallway.

Bob is the star salesman for the company and an all-around good guy. He's an extrovert who tells good jokes. He has a way of talking to people that makes each individual feel valued. But he's also a bit of a rebel and he'll stretch the rules because he knows he's privileged due to his sales ability. Cindy likes Bob and she usually cuts him some slack when he bends the rules.

Now she's having heart palpitations, not in a good way, because she just saw Bob walking down the hall looking like an extra from the set of Magnum, PI. He's wearing a very loud Hawaiian shirt, flip flops, and very short shorts.

Cindy spent two years convincing the socially conservative company president that relaxing the dress code during the summer months would be good for morale. The president only recently accepted the notion that women's work attire can include pant suits or slacks, a concept most companies adopted in the 1990's. To convince him to loosen the rules, she had to create detailed lists of clothing that is appropriate as business casual.

Cindy suspects the president will have an apoplectic fit if he sees Bob's current wardrobe choice. Cindy drops her coffee mug and chases Bob down the hall to invite him into her office for a quiet chat.

What are Cindy's options?

1. She can ask Bob where he bought his clothes so that she can upgrade her husband's wardrobe for their August vacation.
2. She can send Bob home with instructions to change his clothes. Of course, there is no guarantee Bob will follow her instructions or return later today.
3. She can review the business casual definition with Bob and ask why he is not complying with it. She can always hope that he has an acceptable excuse for ignoring the rules.

Business attire standards have relaxed over the years. In some ways, the mark of financial success is to emulate Steve Jobs by wearing black turtlenecks and blue jeans. Employers are struggling to balance the demands of employees for casual attire while maintaining a "professional" image for customers.

Happy Veterans Day!

The Bald Eagle

> This story is a tribute to my cousin Ed, a Vietnam War veteran who served with distinction for 20 years in the U.S. Army. The story originally appeared the week before November 11th.

Cole retired from the Army after 20 years of service with lots of hash marks on his sleeves and medals on his chest for his combat experience. Cole thought he'd enjoy a break from educating second lieutenants on how to stay alive in a combat zone. But six months after he retired his wife ordered him to get a job because he was driving her crazy. A former sergeant can't just sit around the house; he needs to stay busy.

With that encouragement, Cole started a company with a couple of former Army buddies. Since they all loved the uniform they once wore they decided to hire only people with military training. Their small workforce includes men and women who are former military as well as a couple of current members of the National Guard or reserves.

Cole's company is a revolving door for some employees due to deployments to hotspots around the world. As a private sector employer, Cole and his co-owners know they must comply with the Uniformed Services Employment and Re-employment Rights Act (USERRA).

This law requires that military personnel who are called up for active duty must be re-hired by their private sector employers with the same seniority, status and pay as they would have had without the deployment. This law also allows employees and their families to stay on the employer's group health plan while the employees are deployed.

Next week on November 11th, Cole will celebrate Veterans Day by marching in the local town's parade with other veterans. To all the men and women like Cole, happy Veterans Day!

Seasonal Slush And The Office Party

The Wildebeest

> Ah, the joyous holiday season! The best time of year to observe the absurdity of human behavior.
> Yes, I've been to office holiday parties where some of these events happened but for the protection of everyone, I couldn't possibly verify which events I witnessed.
> This was one of my earliest blogs and the reaction to it convinced me to keep writing.

Patricia likes to offer plenty of perks to her employees, including free coffee and tea, catered lunches each quarter, a pool table, and a work-out room. There's only one perk that concerns Patricia: the office holiday party. She can't afford a repeat of last year's fiasco.

Last year some employees enjoyed the wassail and eggnog recipes a little too much. One employee filed a worker comp claim after she fell and broke her arm while trying to dance on the pool table.

Another employee fixated on a colleague's smile and made a highly improper suggestion of how they could spend the rest of the evening. A couple of designated drivers slipped some rum in their cokes and she had to chase them across the parking lot to confiscate their car keys.

Patricia wants her employees to enjoy the season, but there's a limit to what she can tolerate and what her insurance will cover.

What options are available to Patricia?

1. She can cancel the office holiday party based on last year's excesses.
2. She can try to limit her company's liability by requiring all attendees to sign a waiver of liability before attending the party. (She should consult an attorney about this option.)
3. She can build in safeguards, such as limiting the number of drinks allowed to each attendee or holding the event at a hotel and reserving rooms for those who over-indulge.

Every employee has a story about a company holiday party where alcohol resulted in absolutely outrageous behavior. However, many employers have revised their holiday party plans in recognition that the laws have changed regarding a host's liability for drunk driving.

Acknowledgements

Writing a book is not an individual effort by the author. Many others helped on the journey from story ideas to the finished product. That list includes my editor, Kathryn "Kate" Stephenson and my proof-readers, Kellie Graves, Genie Herron, and Susan Hammonds-White. Stephanie Huffman and her team at Epiphany Creative Services (Spencer Besaw, Daniel Brown, Gina Fromm, Melanie Pherson, and Matthew Sklar) took me through their "writer's journey" from concept to published work. Special thanks are also due to the designer, Jonathan Gullery, who transformed my slightly incoherent notations into a creative vision for the book.

Author Biography

Norma Shirk owns Corporate Compliance Risk Advisor, LLC (www.complianceriskadvisor.com), a human resources consultant for employers seeking assistance with HR and employee questions. She also helps employers assess their corporate risks in order to mitigate those risks through internal controls and insurance coverage.

Ms. Shirk earned a J.D. from the University of Tennessee-Knoxville School of Law and a B.A. (History) from Middle Tennessee State University. She holds law licenses in Tennessee, Texas, and Colorado. She transitioned from her career as a lawyer in 2011 and now provides business consulting services.

She speaks frequently on topics ranging from employer responsibilities under the Affordable Care Act, to mitigating corporate risks like employee dishonesty, to the challenges of running a small business. She has presented to the Tennessee Bar Association, Society for Human Resources Management (SHRM) – Middle Tennessee, Clarksville, and Duck River chapters, and the Accounting & Financial Women's Alliance (AFWA) – Music City chapter.

Ms. Shirk has also done military history presentations to the Kiwanis Club, the Andrew Jackson chapter of the Military Officers Association of America (MOAA), and the Brandywine Women's Club. She presents annually to the Breakfast Club of Nashville, most recently on the topic of notable women in history.

Ms. Shirk is the 2016 President of the Breakfast Club of Nashville, a networking group for women professionals, and the former Chair of the Executive Council for the Corporate Counsel Section of the Tennessee Bar Association.

She writes a weekly blog which alternates stories about HR dilemmas available at *HR Compliance Jungle,* www.hrcompliancejungle.com, with stories about heroes and villains in a blog called *History by Norma,* at www.normashirk.com. She is also a founder and monthly contributor to the *Her Savvy* blog, www.hersavvy.com.